Library Service to Children

Putting the Core Competencies to Work

Rosanne Cerny, Penny Markey, and Amanda Williams

Association for Library Service to Children

AMERICAN LIBRARY ASSOCIATION

Composition by ALA Editions in Bookman and Avant Garde using QuarkXpress 5.0 on a PC platform.

Printed on 50-pound white offset, a pH-neutral stock, and bound in 10-point cover stock by Batson Printing.

The paper used in this publication meets the minimum requirements of American National Standard for Information Sciences—Permanence of Paper for Printed Library Materials, ANSI Z39.48-1992. ∞

Library of Congress Cataloging-in-Publication Data

Cerny, Rosanne.
    Outstanding library service to children : putting the core competencies to work / Rosanne Cerny, Penny Markey, Amanda Williams.
        p.   cm.
    Includes bibliographical references and index.
    ISBN 0-8389-0922-1 (alk. paper)
    1. Children's librarians—United States. 2. Children's libraries—United States. 3. Core competencies. I. Markey, Penny. II. Williams, Amanda, 1953-. III. Title.

Z682.4.C49C47 2006
027.62'50973—dc22   2006013188

ISBN-10: 0-8389-0922-1
ISBN-13: 978-0-8389-0922-5

Printed in the United States of America

10   09   08   07   06   1   2   3   4   5

CONTENTS

INTRODUCTION

This book is a companion to *Competencies for Librarians Serving Children in Public Libraries* (1999), published by the Association for Library Service to Children, a division of the American Library Association. *Random House Webster's Collegiate Dictionary* (1997) defines "competence" as "suitable or sufficient skill, knowledge, experience, etc. for some purpose." The ALSC *Competencies* outline a broad range of skills, knowledge, and aptitudes required for those who practice the fine art of children's librarianship. They were first drawn up to highlight and show an appreciation for the wide range of skills children's librarians bring to the table—skills that go far beyond storytelling and puppetry.

The truth of the matter is that children's librarians must provide a much broader array of skills than those few that charm our clientele. We have a rich and varied literature to share with children, but we also need good managerial and technical skills to run our departments, produce web pages, balance budgets, publicize our programs, and more. And we need to be able to do all the other things our colleagues do: material selection, reference service, readers' advisory, and the like. Children's librarians, in fact, are the original multitaskers of the library world.

In order to encourage development of the best combination of skills and professional deportment in our readers and in those they train and supervise, this book presents an expansion of the *Competencies* as a set of best practices with additional background material and resources. We do not aim to write the definitive text on children's librarianship but rather to take a look at the fundamentals and, through supplementary material, to allow librarians to explore and develop their own skills and professional interests as needed. In each chapter we discuss one major competency, giving background information and explaining how that set of skills applies to your job. A bibliography of well-regarded books on the topic is appended to each chapter, so the reader can do further research as needed.

We also hope to provide a text for supervisors and administrators that outlines the philosophy of service, the proud history, and, of course, the skills needed to build an exemplary children's department in their public libraries. Whether that department consists of one frontline librarian or a staff of librarians, paraprofessionals, and other support staff, we need to provide the best customer service, collections, and programs to the children of the community. The children's room also serves the parents, caregivers, teachers, and other adults working with children, but the youngsters must always come first.

In her 1953 book *The Unreluctant Years: A Critical Approach to Children's Literature*, Lillian H. Smith wrote the following:

> Because we are adults so long and childhood is so brief and fleeting, it is assumed that the experience of childhood is relatively so much the less important. Yet childhood is the impressionable and formative period, so receptive and so brief that a child has less need of and less time for the mediocre than an adult. The impressions of childhood are lasting, and the sum of its impressions is the pattern taken on by maturity.

For those of us who work with or raise children, this is a lovely summation of why children always deserve but don't always get the best efforts of the adults who work with them. We respond to Ms. Smith's poetic expression of our own ideal with smiles and nodding heads because we know children are special, and we try to do our best for them in direct provision of service, and as advocates for those within the library or in the larger community.

Another of the "founding mothers" of our profession, Anne Carroll Moore, codified her philosophy into what she called the "Four Respects"—all of which she instilled in the staff she trained at the New York Public Library:

- First, respect for the children
- Second, respect for the books
- Third, respect for the children's librarian as an integral element in the library's organization
- Fourth, and finally, respect for the professional status of children's librarianship

To develop librarians who provide the best service for children, you must begin with people who genuinely like children. Pollyanna need not apply. Children can be annoying, frustrating, loud, messy, and downright unpleasant, and you can put up with them only if, in the end, you just like kids. Not only must you like them, but you should have some educational or psychological training or background to understand the developmental issues that affect children at different ages. You must also interact well with the adults who care for and cater to children. In fact, this is where our competency list must begin, because understanding our customers is the basis of providing good service.

Each of the seven chapters that follow opens by citing the specific competency area covered by that chapter. The discussion then elaborates the points listed, illustrating them with actual policies, procedures, and training materials. Each chapter's comprehensive reading list directs readers to more in-depth sources for their individual self-development plans. The book's appendix lists Internet resources valuable for each competency.

Not every person will be equally good at each facet of the job. It is up to the reader to determine what he or she does well and to recognize which areas need improvement. Make an honest assessment of your strengths and weaknesses and then map out a professional development plan of your own. The reading lists will help you develop your investigations into the various competencies.

We strongly recommend that the new librarian find a mentor who will pass on his or her hard-earned professional tricks of the trade. Or, if you are the trainer of new librarians, we encourage you, in turn, to be a true mentor. Also, become involved with your professional associations at local, state, and national levels to keep yourself interested in new trends and techniques. Continuing education in this field is largely a matter of personal choice: choose to be the best.

For many years, children's librarians were expected to develop managerial and supervisory skills only on the most basic level—just sufficient to run a small department. Few were recognized or rewarded for the skills shared with their adult and reference department colleagues, and often only the largest urban systems offered a real "job ladder" for us. Today, public libraries are recognizing children's librarians as professionals in every sense of the word, and libraries of all sizes have directors, administrators, and managers who came up through the ranks primarily in children's services.

As we've suggested, not every children's librarian will be a superstar in every aspect of the job, but we should all make an attempt to be competent in all of these areas. In this book we explain why these skills are necessities if you are to become a well-rounded professional, whether you spend your career in a small library setting, a series of libraries with growing or changing responsibilities, or a large system.

To paraphrase Robert Fulghum's famous statement in his best-selling *All I Really Need to Know I Learned in Kindergarten* (1988), many library administrators today can say, "Everything I needed to know I learned in the Children's Room."

one

Knowledge
of Client Group

- Understands theories of infant, child, and adolescent learning and development and their implications for library service.

- Recognizes the effects of societal developments on the needs of children.

- Assesses the community regularly and systematically to identify community needs, tastes, and resources.

- Identifies clients with special needs as a basis for designing and implementing services, following American Disabilities Act (ADA) and state and local regulations where appropriate.

- Recognizes the needs of an ethnically diverse community.

- Understands and responds to the needs of parents, care givers, and other adults who use the resources of the children's department.

- Creates an environment in the children's area which provides for enjoyable and convenient use of library resources.

- Maintains regular communication with other agencies, institutions, and organizations serving children in the community.

Understanding the latest in learning and development theories has always been a cornerstone of children's librarianship. Many of these theories have helped shape how library services are delivered today. As late as the 1970s, many libraries did not offer programs for children under four years of age. But as an increasingly educated and demanding group of parents requested service for toddlers and even babies from their local libraries, many public libraries responded, for example, by adding board books and very simple concept books to their collections; offering programs for younger children accompanied by an adult; and developing other services and programs for parents and caregivers. Libraries now routinely offer lap-sit programs for infants, toddler times, traditional story hours for pre-kindergarteners, as well as a wide array of programs for school-age children.

Libraries were not working in a vacuum when they made these changes. Our developmentally appropriate programs were designed to take advantage of the latest and best research from psychologists, educators, and others studying early childhood. Among the findings influencing library responses were these: 80 percent of brain development occurs in the first three years of life; half of what we learn in a lifetime is accomplished by age five; there are strong links between language learning and learning to read. In light of such findings, early childhood programming became more important to families and the educational community, and to libraries.

As more mothers moved into the workforce, and more very young children went into daycare and Headstart programs, libraries adjusted their services and learned from the experts. For example, the ALSC/PLA "Every Child Ready to Read" program included evaluation at each step of its development. "Every Child Ready to Read" also drew on the latest developmental ideas to redesign the delivery of early childhood library programs to be most helpful and relevant to children, parents, and other caregivers—with more attention given to how listening to stories can develop important skills for learning to read.

Research into brain development, speech and reading linkages, and the ability of children of different ages and learning styles to adapt to a learning environment helped the development of the lap-sits, parent modeling, and vocabulary-building formats so popular today. As researchers developed an understanding of the plasticity of babies' brains, they realized that childhood is designed for learning. Children learn through observation, through hearing and other sensory input, and through play. The flexibility of the human brain continues through life, making us the flexible species we are.

Briefly, half a lifetime's learning occurs in the first five years. All the basics, from motor skills to language, develop before a child is ready for kindergarten. The elementary school years, from age six to twelve, see great changes in intellectual development and ability combined with a further refinement of motor skills and changes in children's interests and psychological organization. Middle schoolers are entering the volatile stage of adolescence, which marks the second major spurt of brain growth and development. Combined with hormonal and physical changes, it makes for a stormy but fascinating passage for children and the adults around them.

To plan and present programs or develop collections appropriately, a children's librarian needs to understand the developmental needs and differences of each age group served. The librarian also needs to be on sure ground to deflect the "but my child is gifted" parent who doesn't understand why there are specific age or developmental limits to programs, computer use policy, and other services.

School-age children's reading and research needs and abilities change greatly from one stage to the next. When building collections or providing reference help or readers' advisory, the librarian must be able to assess more than reading level to serve the child well. Similarly, computer skills vary widely by age. The librarian must recognize and take into account fine motor development, how children focus on a screen's design, and other developmental factors when designing websites, reviewing software, and guiding computer research.

Children's librarians also work with a variety of adults with very different levels of understanding or training about children. Even a barely literate parent or caregiver may have a more practical and intuitive understanding of a child's stages of growth than a school or library administrator with advanced degrees. Parents always want the best for their children. When we provide workshops or model simple learning activities for them, they are a very receptive audience. Professionals, on the other hand, may have concentrated their educations on specialized subject areas and may not always understand how developmental differences affect children's access and internalization of information, for example. Since we librarians generally work with a wider age spectrum than most educators, we can often provide some guidance to them, too—especially in areas of our own expertise, such as what kids like to read or how they use computers. Children's librarians must, then, act as advocates for the children and their needs when working with other adults.

Librarians also should be aware of the service they can provide in advancing research into early childhood learning. Local universities may provide your library student researchers to help with formal evaluations being conducted for grants or reports, and perhaps you can refer families to their formal research studies. Library journals also welcome "best practices" articles on innovative programs, especially when they cover problems that must be overcome to present the new activity successfully.

As medicine and the other life sciences, psychology, education, and other social sciences continue to investigate the developmental stages of childhood, librarians must make an effort to stay abreast with new developments and continue to adapt traditional library services to new best practices. Similarly, as other issues in education arise, such as science literacy, librarians must adapt their program goals to include ways of introducing new material into programming.

4

The librarian and the library's clientele are products of the social change that is always with us. As baby boomer moms return to the workforce, or as new immigration trends sweep a city, children and families are affected—and therefore the children's room and librarian are also affected. Because we see the effects of new trends firsthand, we can also be strong advocates in the community for adaptations to change. In our own practices, we can help smooth the change with new programs and services, make our collections more responsive to the lives children actually live, and become a vital resource and clearinghouse of programs and services available in our communities to parents and other child-serving adults who need the information.

It is important for your own job satisfaction to understand why and how children react to you and your services. Ask for feedback from them or their adults, and use it to improve your services and skills. Libraries may chose to use formal user surveys, focus groups, or more casual conversational feedback from individual customers. The important part of the process is to understand if the materials and services you offer match the needs of your library's customers.

The children's librarian must not only understand children's developmental stages and how they relate to both formal and informal education but also make an effort to reach out to teachers and administrators. When building your collection, be familiar with the curricular requirements of the students who use your facility. Work proactively with adult customers to help them understand the variety of options available to children at each grade level, since we know that children progress at greatly different rates.

Be sensitive to children and adults with learning or reading difficulties, and to those with cultural backgrounds different from your own. Take an intelligent interest in the demographic changes taking place around you, and act to create a welcoming environment for newcomers. Through community contacts, actively recruit new customers to the library.

Working with other service providers in the community not only gives the library greater visibility but also promotes its value to the community and brings in feedback from supporters for improvements in service. Regular participation in these larger, more diverse committees or working groups provides another informal way of regularly surveying for needed changes. Other municipal departments or nongovernmental organizations will experience changes in the community in terms of their particular expertise, whether police, social service, health care, or educational; the library can pick up clues and new perspectives from all these partners, and also act as a clearinghouse of information for professionals and community members.

The Child Development Table provided here is used at the Queens (New York) Library to introduce new librarians to the basic stages of child development. It synthesizes a great deal of research from numerous sources and is expanded from an appendix to *The Key to the Future: Revised Minimum Standards for Youth Services in Public Libraries of New York State* (1994).

CHILD DEVELOPMENT TABLE		
PHYSICAL GROWTH AND LEARNING STYLES	PSYCHOLOGICAL DEVELOPMENT	LIBRARY APPLICATIONS
Infancy, ages 0–2		
Single greatest stage of physiological growth and development, centered on development of motor skills, early language, and learning through sensory input.	Egocentric and family-oriented; explores the world through eyes, ears, hands, feet, and mouth. Parents must be encouraged to be the child's first teacher.	Time to begin reading aloud to children (board books, Mother Goose and other nursery rhymes); enjoys listening to music and responds to rhythmic sounds. Lap-sit programs most appropriate. Modeling for parents an important part of programming.

PHYSICAL GROWTH AND LEARNING STYLES	PSYCHOLOGICAL DEVELOPMENT	LIBRARY APPLICATIONS
Toddlers, ages 2–3		
Beginning to refine physical skills and taking first steps to independence.	Begins to assert self. Understands simple concepts. Begins to understand sequences and simple cause and effect. Play still basically independent of others.	Enjoys concept books, lift-the-flap and cumulative or repetitive stories. Listens to simple stories but still needs much physical activity and one-on-one interaction. Programs should include caregiver.
Preschool, ages 4–5		
Language skills fully in place, vocabulary expanding rapidly. Playful stage of language, enjoys nonsense rhymes and versifying. Sequencing, spatial relationships, and other basic mathematical skills developing.	Begins to explore the world beyond the nuclear family. Begins to identify with other children. Imaginative play at its peak.	Can follow directions, sit still for longer stories and activities, and do simple craft activities. Most, but not all, children comfortable attending programs independently.
Primary grades, K–2		
Logical reasoning begins. Schoolwork concentrates on the "3 Rs." Hands-on learning critical.	The "3 Cs" develop: calculation, consolidation, and cooperation. Asks lots of questions and enjoys working in groups. Personal life experiences dominate the view of the world.	Beginning readers themselves, they enjoy being read to. More sophisticated sense of humor and a wider variety of stories appreciated.

(Cont'd)

CHILD DEVELOPMENT TABLE (Cont'd)		
PHYSICAL GROWTH AND LEARNING STYLES	PSYCHOLOGICAL DEVELOPMENT	LIBRARY APPLICATIONS
Middle grades, 3–5		
Beginning of independent academics and complex reasoning. Enjoys collecting things and beginning hobbies.	Expanding sense of individuality, but with the sense of self more influenced by relationships outside of the immediate family.	Ready for a full range of library programs, from formal storytelling to fairly difficult crafts, to lectures and demonstrations of personal interest. Moving into chapter books and materials for independent study.
Preadolescents ("tweens"), grades 6–8		
Onset of puberty. Able to handle abstract reasoning. Research and study skills advance with increased organization and self-discipline.	Self-conscious, beginning to challenge authority, but still dependent on the family. Identifies more with teenagers than children. Becoming socially and civically aware; may begin to volunteer in the community.	Can use the full range of reference material, may occasionally use the young adult or adult collections. Developing an interest in popular culture and peer recommendations for reading.
Adolescents, grades 9–12		
Final spurt of brain development. Major hormonal changes occurring, physical development basically complete. Integrating formal learning into more independent lifestyles.	Often seems to be a child in an adult's body, but ready to become a fully participating member of the larger community. Can be almost as self-centered as a toddler, or thoroughly altruistic and thoughtful of others.	The young adult collection is a bridge into the adult collection, although age-specific materials and programs still essential. Need spaces of their own as well as interactions with staff who recognize their growing independence.

This chapter's reading list will take you to publications that offer far more in-depth information on these stages and how they affect service to children. Most of the sources listed for "Programming Skills" offer information on why and how to tailor library programs to the various age groups.

Obviously, good children's service includes well-selected and maintained collections of books and other media, but it also requires a welcoming physical space that reflects the variety of children's use patterns and the different ages served. At the most basic level, the physical space should include furniture variously sized for different age groups—low shelves, seats, and tables in the area for younger customers, for example. Larger furniture is more comfortable for older children, and they can reach higher ranges of shelves. Bright colors; bulletin boards to display posters or other items of interest to children; a separate meeting space for storytimes, class visits, or craft programs; perhaps informal seating arrangements for parents and children to share stories—all of these make the children's room an inviting area of the library, and they are not necessarily expensive to design into new construction or renovation plans.

Signage with large, easily read letters or readily recognized symbols and design elements that attract children can be added along with minor facility renovations. Making a special area that is safe for the youngest children should be a priority, but the middle schoolers should be considered as well. As they move closer to adolescence, this group will want to distance themselves from the "little kids," literally and figuratively. More sophisticated decoration, more suitable furniture, and other age-related factors help differentiate their area(s) within the larger area. Likewise, if the library has a youth services area, another space tailored for teens should be designed to suit their needs.

During the design of new buildings or major renovations, a wise administrator includes the children's librarian on the design advisory team. Professionals from other disciplines often do not understand the need for flexibility and practical considerations of running a library. Having the right practitioners on the advisory team will, in the long run, result in a more satisfactory working and public service space.

Suggested Reading

Benne, M. 1991. Audiences to be served. In *Principles of children's services in public libraries*, 2–28. Chicago: American Library Association.   JR 027.625 (HQ)

———. 1991. Planning facilities. In *Principles of children's services in public libraries*, 152–192. Chicago: American Library Association.

Brazelton, T. B., and S. I. Greenspan. 2000. *The irreducible needs of children: What every child must have to grow, learn, and flourish.* Cambridge, MA: Perseus.   649.1 CA G LA MI MH SA WD

Bredekamp, S., and C. Copple. 1997. *Developmentally appropriate practice in early childhood programs*, rev. ed. Washington, DC: National Association for the Education of Young Children.   305.231   (63-CU) (93- CA G LA MI SA)

Erikson, E. 1963. *Childhood and society.* New York: W. W. Norton.

Fasick, A. M. 1998. Planning facilities. In *Managing children's services in the public library*, 2d ed., 135–150. Englewood, CO: Libraries Unlimited.

Feinberg, S., K. Deerr, B. Jordan, M. Byrine, and L. Kropp. 2006. *Family-centered library handbook.* New York: Neal-Schuman.   JR 027.625 (CA)

Feinberg, S., J. E. Kuchner, and S. Feldman. 1998. *Learning environments for young children: Rethinking library spaces and services.* Chicago: American Library Association.

Greene, E. 1991. *Books, babies and libraries: Serving infants, toddlers, their parents, and caregivers.* Chicago: American Library Association.

Michaels, A., and D. Michaels. 1996. *Library buildings, equipment, and the ADA: Compliance issues and solutions.* Chicago: American Library Association.   022.3166 (HQ)

Piaget, J. 1958. *The origins of intelligence in children.* New York: International Universities Press. 155.413 - LA MI SA

Smith, P. K., H. Cowie, and M. Blades. 2003. *Understanding children's development.* Malden, MA: Blackwell.

Steele, A. T. 2001. Knowing your clientele. In *Bare bones children's services: Tips for public library generalists,* 1–11. Chicago: American Library Association. JR 027.625 HQ - au

Sullivan, M. 2005. *Fundamentals of children's services.* Chicago: American Library Association. JR 027.625 (HQ)

Tarwick-Smith, J. 1997. *Early childhood development: A multicultural perspective.* Englewood Cliffs, NJ: Prentice-Hall.

Walling, L. L., and M. H. Karrenbrock. 1993. *Disabilities, children in libraries: Mainstreaming services in public libraries and school media centers.* Englewood, CO: Libraries Unlimited.

Walter, V. A. 2001. *Children and libraries: Getting it right.* Chicago: American Library Association. JR 627.625

two

Administrative and Management Skills

- Participates in all aspects of the library's planning process to represent and support children's services.

- Sets long- and short-range goals, objectives, and priorities.

- Analyzes the costs of library services to children in order to develop, justify, administer/manage, and evaluate a budget.

- Writes job descriptions and interviews, trains, encourages continuing education, and evaluates staff who work with children, consulting with other library administrations as indicated in library personnel policy.

- Demonstrates problem-solving, decision making, and mediation techniques.

- Delegates responsibility appropriately and supervises staff constructively.

- Documents and evaluates services.

- Identifies outside sources of funding and writes effective grant applications.

- Applies appropriate tools to implement and facilitate management functions.

S torytimes, craft programs, colorful, attractive décor that wel-
comes children, good relationships with local schools and
community involvement: What more could a director expect?
Excellent managerial and administrative skills are as vital to
the youth services department as they are to the library as a
whole. It is critical that a children's librarian be an excellent
manager of resources as well as a valued member of the
library's management team. A library's administration has the
same expectations of managerial efficiency, service delivery,
and customer satisfaction for the children's department, whatever the size or configuration, as it has for the other public
service departments in the organization.

In addition, the children's librarians are generally responsible for more original programming than other departments.
They are involved in outreach to schools, networking with other
child-serving organizations in the community, and advocating
for children and their caregivers as library customers. With
such a wide range of activity, the children's library must be well
organized and efficient.

But that's only a small part of the picture. Every children's
librarian should be able to manage a budget as well as cam-
paign for more and better resources, space, and other tools for
his department. He should know and observe the policy and
procedure set by the library's administration. Beyond that, a
wise department manager should also aim to be a "player" in
the development of that policy and procedure, especially where
children's needs are directly addressed. Unless the children's
librarian acts as advocate, those needs may not always be routinely considered.

Skills of advocacy, coupled with managerial competence,
are key in making your department a respected and integral
part of the library or system. Without these skills, you may not
be taken as seriously as other department heads when it's time
to provide input into strategic planning, budget, or other managerial discussions.

Achieving excellence in providing public service or in fulfilling your managerial responsibilities rests on a solid foundation of planning. Planning is a way of looking toward a goal and integrating all aspects of service to achieve it. You may be planning a day-by-day activity, a short-term process, or long-range strategy. Although many people find planning difficult, especially for the long term, the figure below breaks down the process into just four essential elements. This model can be used for a one-time action plan (e.g., weed the picture books), as a way of perfecting a more ambitious plan (e.g., booking a new program, assessing the results, reconfiguring it until you find a program that really works for your audience), or for long-term strategic planning.

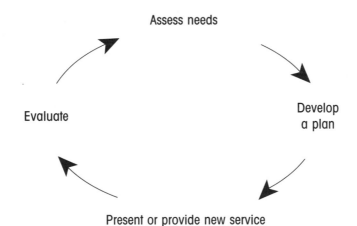

Planning always begins with a needs assessment. This, in its simplest form, implies looking around and identifying what needs to be done. Such a process may be as simple as starting systematic weeding at one end of the room and going to the other, or as complicated as designing a whole new children's room or plan of service. The complexity of the project influences the level of study and planning needed.

After identifying needs, you develop an action plan. What are you going to do? What practical steps must you accomplish to put the plan into action? Don't forget the resources needed and budget required.

The third step is to put the plan into action, and the fourth is to evaluate it. If the evaluation is positive, the project is complete. Evaluations vary, depending on the project. Your eye will tell you if the new display is attractive; circulation will tell you if customers notice and borrow the materials. Comments from an audience help you self-evaluate a program, but you may need customer surveys or focus groups to evaluate a new service thoroughly. You may even need longitudinal studies to evaluate long-term projects or those with elaborate or hard-to-measure outcomes, like literacy preparedness.

If the evaluation process shows that there are problems with the plan of service or project, it's time to reassess, develop a new plan, take action again, and reevaluate—as many times as needed to perfect the new service. Graphically, the cycle becomes a continuous spiral, until you can declare success.

There are a variety of different planning processes that work in different circumstances. Most important is that the process help you develop priorities of service, allowing you to make decisions based on the available facts. The plan provides a roadmap to how to achieve the intended result, including how much time, staff, and other resources it will take. It also forces you to evaluate, formally or informally, how the plan and the process for achieving it has worked. Planning should force you to think about what you are doing and why, and how to move deliberately toward your goal.

In your managerial role, it is always wise to have written policies and procedures. If your library already has a policy manual, you and the children's room staff should obviously be familiar with and adhere to it. There may be situations that require you to adapt library policies or procedures to the specific needs of children. In such circumstances, you should communicate any changes to supervisors, and make sure you have their approval. These approved changes should then be formally incorporated into library policy.

Your library or department may also need a mission statement—a brief, concise expression of the library's or department's purpose and place in the community. A mission statement provides direction to staff and serves as a basis for planning, and it should be carefully worded and precise. A library's mission statement is a mandate for service, and it should apply equally to all library departments. A department's mission statement may also be used to formalize or define its service population, scope of collections, or other hallmarks that make the department special.

Other basic policies every library should have in writing include membership or card registration, book and media selection, circulation rules, customer service policies (including rules for behavior), human resources policies, and other action items approved by the board of directors. These are vital for training staff, handling complaints from the public with fairness and consistency, and maintaining good employee relations.

Also recommended, but often overlooked, is a strategic plan—a document that attempts to anticipate the library's future needs and plots a course toward an ideal vision. A strategic plan should be based on a solid understanding of the community—its demographics, political structure, and economic capacity to support the library. A good strategic plan will be based in part on community input. What do your customers need and want? Are you trying to be all things to all people, or a consistent, necessary community service that is not provided by other organizations? What can the community, and therefore the library, afford? A strategic plan is essential for long-range planning, and it may be required by some municipal or state library regulatory units.

Effective planning requires knowledge of the community being served; awareness of the resources that can be applied (budget, staff, space); and collaboration between community partners and staff members. Additionally, depending on the situation, your strategic plan may include a marketing plan, an evaluation strategy (including cost-benefit analysis), or knowledge of the competition. Why, for example, offer an afterschool homework program if the school down the street has free tutoring, or if the Boys and Girls Club has free recreational and educational programs every day?

Your community may be a neighborhood, a municipality, or some other political or geographic unit; it may be a defined subset such as children, teens, or preschoolers. However it is defined, learn your community's demographic makeup. You can find this information in documents like census or city planning reports, but you should also get out into the community to find the underserved populations as well.

As a department manager, you should know what resources are already available, or what your projected needs will be if you are in budget negotiations, for example. You may also have to negotiate for use of a meeting room, or for extra support staff to check out books after a program or class visit. No one likes unpleasant surprises, and that includes your managerial colleagues.

Effective planning will help you show the library administration that you are regularly evaluating the programs, collections, and other services under your direction. If the costs are high but you feel the service is valuable, learn how to use your planning and evaluation to frame your arguments. For example, your infant and caregiver programs must be of limited size because of developmental issues. But if you have a large population of young mothers, especially from economically disenfranchised families, you can use the educational research you put into your programs to make a powerful argument for their need. The administration can in turn argue what an important value-added service this is for the community to the political powers-that-be.

Many grants require community collaboration. Have you made the connections to other child-serving organizations in your community? How open is the communication among the staff of the library? Can you develop collaborations in-house that serve the children's needs?

In large libraries, there may be foundations to help raise money, public relations departments to do the marketing, or other internal departments to help write grant proposals, design evaluations, and other necessary documents. In smaller libraries, you may have to do these tasks yourself. If library school did not prepare you for these responsibilities, consult this chapter's reading list and start reading.

Another area that is likely to involve you is budget planning. Depending on the size of your library or scope of your job, this responsibility too may vary. At the very least, as a department manager you should know how much disposable budget you need for books and other materials, and how much staff you need to provide your services. And you need to be able to justify your requests. Costs may include the funds, staff time, and energy necessary for printing, publicity, mailings, arts and crafts supplies, and summer reading club incentives, to name just a few.

A good manager is a good communicator. Those who believe "knowledge is power" and hang onto information jealously will not, in the long run, be effective managers or supervisors. Keep your supervisors, colleagues, and staff apprised of what is happening. Share information formally (in reports, staff meetings) and informally (over coffee). Be professional but friendly and approachable. Develop a collegial attitude with all levels of staff—each of us has skills and knowledge that are vital to the total effort, and you never know in this small world when a pleasant attitude will repay you and your department in kind.

A good manager is able to perform and teach a wide variety of skills. Rotate job assignments and cross-train staff; it helps them stay fresh and invigorated. Ask those who are particularly good at early childhood programs, for example, to share their expertise and train colleagues.

As a supervisor, you can affect the morale of your staff by letting people be accountable for specific projects or programs and by giving positive feedback, or at least detached criticism that concentrates on performance, not personality. No one likes surprises on an evaluation. If a situation needs correcting, a private conference with constructive criticism at the time of the problem is always preferable to a formal written evaluation months after the event.

To be a true team player, be a problem solver, be interested in the "big picture," and learn from any more experienced librarian willing to mentor you—and, in turn, mentor others.

Suggested Reading

Anderson, C. 2001. *Write grants, get money.* Worthington, OH: Linworth.

Association for Library Service to Children, Association for Library Trustees and Advocates, and Public Library Association. 2002. *Unattended children in the public library: A resource guide.* Chicago: American Library Association.

Ball, S., comp. 2003. *Know kidding: The best of the best in youth services.* Wheeling, IL: North Suburban Library System.

Benne, M. 1991. Children's librarian as manager. In *Principles of children's services in public libraries,* 29–65. Chicago: American Library Association.

Bielefield, A., and L. Cheeseman. 2006. *Technology and copyright law.* New York: Neal-Schuman.

Byrd, S. M. 2005. *¡Benvenidos! ¡welcome!: A handy resource guide for marketing your library to Latinos.* Chicago: American Library Association.

Connor, J. G. 1990. *Children's services handbook.* Phoenix, AZ: Oryx.

Cruse, C., and M. Cart, eds. 2002. *Children's services training manual.* Willows, CA: North State Cooperative Library System.

Fasick, A. M. 1998. Developing policies and procedures. In *Managing children's services in the public library,* 2d ed., 1–11. Englewood, CO: Libraries Unlimited.

———. 1998. Developing tools to meet program goals. In *Managing children's services in the public library*, 2d ed., 13–21. Englewood, CO: Libraries Unlimited.

———. 1998. Fund-raising activities. In *Managing children's services in the public library*, 2d ed., 165–174. Englewood, CO: Libraries Unlimited.

———. 1998. Preparing budgets. In *Managing children's services in the public library*, 2d ed., 127–134. Englewood, CO: Libraries Unlimited.

———. 1998. Recruiting and retaining staff. In *Managing children's services in the public library*, 2d ed., 51–62. Englewood, CO: Libraries Unlimited.

Gerding, S. R., and P. H. Mackellar. 2006. *Grants for libraries.* New York: Neal-Schuman.

Hall-Ellis, S. D., and F. W. Hoffmann. 1999. *Grantsmanship for small libraries and school library media centers.* Englewood, CO: Libraries Unlimited.

Hallam, A. W., and T. R. Dalston. 2005. *Managing budgets and finances.* New York: Neal-Schuman.

Larson, J., and H. Totten. 1998. *Model policies for small and medium public libraries.* New York: Neal-Schuman.

Nelson, S. 2001. *The new planning for results: A streamlined approach.* Chicago: American Library Association.

Nelson, S., E. Altman, and D. Mayo. 2000. *Managing for results: Effective resource allocation for public libraries.* Chicago: American Library Association.

Nelson, S., and J. Garcia. 2003. *Creating policies for results: From chaos to clarity.* Chicago: American Library Association.

New York Library Association, Youth Services Section. 1990. *Kids welcome here: Writing public library policies that promote use by young people.* Albany, NY: New York Library Association.

———. 2004. *Kids still welcome here! An update of public library policies that promote use by young people.* Albany, NY: New York Library Association.

Pfeil, A. B. 2005. *Going places with youth outreach: Smart marketing strategies for your library.* Chicago: American Library Association.

Rhea, J. R. 2005. *Demonstrating results: Using outcome measurement in your library.* Chicago: American Library Association.

Sullivan, M. 2005. *Fundamentals of children's services.* Chicago: American Library Association.

Swan, J. 2002. *Fundraising for libraries: 25 proven ways to get more money for your library.* New York: Neal-Schuman.

Taft Group. 2005. *Big book of library grant money 2006: Profiles of private and corporate foundations and direct corporate givers receptive to library grant proposals.* Chicago: American Library Association.

Trotta, M. 2006. *Supervising staff.* New York: Neal-Schuman.

U.S. Department of Commerce. National Telecommunications and Information Administration. 2003. Children's Internet Protection Act, Pub. L. 106-554 [electronic resource]: study of technology protection measures in 1703; report to Congress. Washington, DC: Department of Commerce, National Telecommunications and Information Administration.

Walter, V. A. 1992. *Output measures for public library service to children: A manual for standardized procedures.* Chicago: American Library Association.

———. 2001. *Children and libraries: Getting it right.* Chicago: American Library Association.

three

Communication Skills

- Defines and communicates the needs of children so that administrators, other library staff, and members of the larger community understand the basis for children's services.

- Demonstrates interpersonal skills in meeting with children, parents, staff, and community.

- Adjusts to the varying demands of writing planning documents, procedures, guidelines, press releases, memoranda, reports, grant applications, annotations, and reviews in all formats, including print and electronic.

- Speaks effectively when addressing individuals, as well as small and large groups.

- Applies active listening skills.

- Conducts productive formal and informal reference interviews.

- Communicates constructively with "problem patrons."

In chapter 2 we touched upon the importance of good communication skills in a children's services manager, but in many ways all librarians need to be good listeners and good communicators. In this chapter we explore how you can use your knowledge and understanding of children to facilitate your advocacy role, but also to perform daily activities like providing reference and readers' advisory services and enforcing discipline. Children's librarians have good verbal skills for presenting children's programs, but they are often quite effective public speakers for adult groups too, and effective interacting with patrons of any age. (We address public speaking and storytelling skills from other perspectives in chapter 5: Programming Skills).

Good written communications reflect well on the library as well as on the staff member who does the writing. Reports to the administration, grant proposals and progress reports, public relations or marketing documents, reviews and correspondence on paper or electronic formats—these all have a wide reach. They need to be carefully composed, concise, and businesslike. You *will* be graded for grammar and spelling.

But writing and speaking are only part of the picture of effective communications. Active listening is also an asset, privately and professionally. Active listening shows that you are paying attention to what another person is saying. It requires you to ask leading questions that help you understand the other person's needs. When you are doing floorwork, either reference or readers' advisory, it is an essential skill for good service provision. Library customers may often be unclear in their own minds about what they are searching for. A good reference interview allows them to clarify their needs, gives you as much information as possible, and in the long run saves time for both of you. The reference interview should clarify for you and the customer what the latter really wants. Does he want a history of World War II or just pictures of tanks and planes? Does the Harry Potter fan want more fantastics, or books over 400 pages long, or coming-of-age stories? Careful questioning narrows your search parameters. Knowledge of the collection helps you zero in on the most appropriate materials to recommend.

There are many times when, formally or informally, you are required to take on an advocacy role for children or children's services. Intervening on behalf of a shy child whose parent is doing all of the talking in a reference interview, for example, empowers the child to speak on her own behalf. When you are working with colleagues on policy or budgetary issues, a good presentation on behalf of your department's needs and issues will certainly be required. Likewise, as a professional working with children, you may be invited to give public testimony to political or educational bodies or media outlets on behalf of the library or the children in your community.

In all cases, you will be called upon to interpret children's library needs and communicate them to others. Clear, concise, grammatical, easily understandable English, whether oral or written, is a requirement. Passion for your subject may be implied, but a rational exposition will garner more attention and respect. Remember the "pediatric conundrum." Your audience must respect you for working with children, not expect you to act like a kid because you do. Your goal is to be perceived as an expert adult, not a child in high heels.

It is also important to develop political and tactical skills to enhance your advocacy role. Every organization, even a small library with only a few employees and a small board of trustees, has political undercurrents within, and also needs to deal with real political forces in the community. Learning to negotiate the social and political scene without inadvertently creating enemies or critics is vital to an effective working environment. Honing your diplomatic skills and rising above interdepartmental conflicts go a long way toward engaging the attention and respect of others, regardless of the political climate.

In any case, politics is not necessarily negative. Being "politic" means exercising one's shrewdness or prudence in a tactful, diplomatic way. A politically astute person within an organization understands where the centers of power lie, and how to approach them to benefit herself or her department. Sometimes being politic also means knowing how to make an impressive case or how to make a deal that works both for a department's benefit and the success of the larger organization.

Now that we've explored the importance of good communication for the children's librarians, let's look at some specific areas with an eye to strengthening communication.

Written Communication

There are several different circumstances in which you will be called on to express yourself in a written format. Some situations call for a more formal style, some may allow a more casual, conversational style. Here are some key areas where a children's librarian may be required to write.

Professional reporting about your department. Written reports—whether to the library board or administration, as part of grant proposals or progress reports, or for media release—require concise, businesslike language. Professionally composed reports always reflect well on your department. If there is a specific required outline or series of questions, don't fudge. Follow the directions or guidelines as required. Find a way to relate your successes or problems in a way that matches the required format.

Grant proposals. To write a good grant proposal, remember that it is crucial to find the right match with a funding source. When foundations or corporations donate money, they want to be sure the recipient (in this case the library) will use the money to further their own mission in the community. Many proposal outlines ask specific questions. When writing your proposal, you must develop a plan or programmatic design that fits both the library's needs and what the funding agency is willing and able to give. You will also have to develop evaluations and reports that satisfy the agency's requirements and expectations. Again, clarity, concise descriptions, and proper, understandable, jargon-free English are required. Also keep in mind that many organizations, even ones that look favorably on libraries, do not thoroughly understand what libraries do. Provide them with some context to show how your project fits into the larger picture of library service to the community. If possible, explain why this new project will be an added value for your customers.

Communicating with superiors. When preparing reports that go up the supervisory chain, learn how to convey negative information in positive terms. For example, if you didn't see the expected growth of registrations for the summer reading club, but more children stuck with the program all summer, focus your evaluation on the completion ratio, the number of books read, or certificates distributed. Don't let your report sound like a carping session, or it will be ignored. Include information on what positive fixes have been attempted. Take a proactive approach where ever possible, but don't be afraid to use the opportunity to inform supervisors that a problem does exist and that you are seeking solutions.

Writing for the profession. Librarians look to one another to solve problems or look at situations with fresh eyes. Take advantage of the opportunities to get in print. Library periodicals are always on the lookout for "best practices" articles, and it is not difficult to write up a program and get it published. Again, clear and concise is best.

Another way to contribute to the professional literature is as a reviewer. Book and media reviews require critical skill and may require you to use a specific format—so check with the publisher.

Writing for the public. Many librarians are asked by local media to prepare regular or occasional columns about library events, suggestions for popular reading, and other information about which librarians have expertise. An expository style that amuses and intrigues the reader may be called for. Writing for a newspaper or other media outlet often gives you the chance to work with an editor. Take advantage of the editor's advice, and use your improved style to spice up more mundane required writing if you can.

Networking

When looking for solutions to new problems, networking with other librarians can be helpful. Whether it is other colleagues in the building or in local, state, or national professional organizations, it is helpful to share information and find out what others are doing in similar situations.

Because we are often separated from colleagues by distance, we tend to reinvent the wheel unnecessarily. Adapting other people's solutions to your own needs can be a quick fix for a problem but can also take advantage of whatever evaluation and revision your colleagues discovered in handling the situation. Sharing information frankly with others is a simple way to become a valuable member of your network. No one appreciates getting a treasured recipe with a key ingredient deliberately left out. If you expect to get good advice from your colleagues, be prepared to give in honest measure.

In this era of electronic communication, joining electronic discussion lists or blogs can be a new way to take advantage of networks. Attending conferences and becoming active in discussion groups or on committees can also be very rewarding.

Public Speaking

Preparing to speak before groups can be just as daunting as learning to write businesslike prose. Before giving a presentation, you should ask yourself the following: What is the purpose of my speech? Who is in the audience? What message do I want to convey? How long should I speak? Should I write my presentation out word-for-word or use an outline?

There is no reason to be nervous about talking to groups of adults. If you can keep a group of squirming three-year-olds engaged for half an hour, you can certainly prepare a ten-minute speech for the town planning board, a half-hour presentation for the PTA, or whatever is needed. Use the same public speaking skills you use in children's programs. Keep eye contact, modulate your voice, use visual aids sparingly to get maximum effect, and when in doubt, KISS (Keep It Simple, Stupid!) works best.

Use the same rules of thumb you use in preparing written reports: be clear, keep to the subject, and as much as possible frame your message around what the particular group has requested or needs to hear. Don't try to be cute unless you are expected to be entertaining. Again, remember the pediatric conundrum, and suit the presentation to the audience.

Nonverbal Communication

Learning to communicate nonverbally is important when dealing with any customers, but particularly with children. Here are some key areas to consider.

Am I approachable? For most children, approaching an unfamiliar adult for help is difficult. If you look too involved in reading, writing, or working on the computer, they will be hesitant to interrupt. If you smile, if you initiate contact with them on the floor, and if you keep your desk clear of piles of books or papers that would serve as an obstruction, children feel more at ease approaching you. Be alert to children who may be hovering nearby but afraid to initiate contact. Ask if you can help them or if they are finding what they need. Other forms of body language may be off-putting to some customers. If you think there may be a problem, consult another staff member you trust to make suggestions on how your body language could be interfering with customer service.

Am I sensitive to cultural differences? Our culture influences how we react to others. In the American culture, we expect people to look each other in the eye during a conversation. Children of some cultures are taught that eye contact is something for adults only, that they should not boldly look an adult or other authority figure directly in the eye. When they don't look directly at you, they are not being shifty, they are being respectful. Ask your friends or colleagues from other ethnic groups if there are special kinds of interactions to expect, to avoid, or to cultivate with members of their group. In some groups, touch may be taboo for people outside the family, or there may be other physical barriers a member of that community can teach you.

With the caveat noted above, it is generally important to establish eye contact. This can be vital in interactions with shy children, or with those who have an overbearing companion who wants to do all the talking. This is why most children's room service desks are lower than adult service desks—so the child can see and be seen by the adults they are dealing with.

Do I command respect? The difference between a little noise and silliness exploding into a serious disciplinary situation may be affected by nonverbal hints the kids pick up from their librarian. Just as animals smell fear and menace a person who is already afraid of them, children sense when adults are reluctant to take control of a situation. They may push the limits just to see what they can get away with, which brings us to another area of communication—rules.

Rules and Discipline

As the person in charge of the children's room, you should set limits, define expectations, and maintain decorum. Each librarian has to develop his own style. Some have "the look"—also developed by teachers, parents, and other authority figures—that let's children know they are in danger of going too far. Others make effective use of the old "I'm letting you know, if I have to come over to this table again . . ." speech. Whatever behavior modification approach works for you, the important thing is that the children know that, when you deliver a threat, you will follow through. If children are told to leave the library for the afternoon for disciplinary reasons, inform your colleagues so they don't inadvertently let the disciplined youth take refuge in another department. If you threaten to call school or family, do it. If you do not follow through and get the reputation of being a pushover, it will be difficult, if not impossible, for you to maintain control thereafter. If you set strict standards, you can always loosen up, but if you begin the school year, or a new job, as an "easy touch," you will find it very hard to later shift gears and become more demanding.

It is important to keep in mind that, though you may be unhappy with a child's behavior on a given day, that child deserves your future support and respect—and another chance. One significant difference between public libraries and schools is that libraries do not keep records from year to year. We librarians try to judge behavior on a day-to-day basis. Children and teens appreciate fairness and respond to it well.

Being a fair but firm disciplinarian shouldn't conflict with your approachability or friendliness toward patrons. Children grow to respect and like adults who maintain a little separation, and most like to know that there are limits to their behavior in a public place. Some young librarians make the mistake of wanting to be "just one of the kids." It is difficult to enforce the rules as "one of the gang," but an adult with a friendly, pleasant attitude or "hip" personality can still be accepted by kids while maintaining the distance necessary to be the role model of proper library behavior.

The library and the librarian should have definite rules about patron behavior. As with other areas open to interpretation, written guidelines are best, but such rules usually deal only with worst-case scenarios. As the person in charge, you can set the limits for acceptable behavior (e.g., moderate voices, no running indoors, speaking in turn) in simple but firm language. Children learn quickly which behavior is acceptable and will generally comply.

We know there are children who like to test the limits, and

for them one must take a firmer stand. Still, it is important to be fair and evenhanded. Give children a chance to modify their behavior—up to a point. If things are getting out of hand, separate the instigators, make them leave the library for a specific length of time if necessary, bring in other staff to help monitor the situation, or whatever works best for the situation. Behavior that is unsafe or puts others in jeopardy must never be tolerated.

It is ironic, but true, that some of the best disciplinarians are neither physically imposing nor particularly scary. They are people who project self-discipline and an honesty that children respond to with respect. Children also respect authority figures who apply rules equally to everyone, including adult patrons. Children are concrete thinkers. When they observe adults playing favorites with one group over another, they not only resent those adults for being unfair but also often deliberately flaunt rules or indulge in naughtiness to annoy them.

How librarians and support staff treat their young customers has a direct impact on how those youngsters will perceive libraries and librarians for a lifetime. Children deserve as much consideration and attention as other patrons, sometimes more. Remember, it only takes fourteen facial muscles to smile, but seventy-two to frown.

Suggested Reading

Christopher, C. 2003. *Empowering your library: A guide to improving service, productivity, and participation.* Chicago: American Library Association.

Cruse, C., and M. Cart, eds. 2002. *Children's services training manual.* Willows, CA: North State Cooperative Library System.

Customer service: More than a smile. 1991. 13 min. videocassette. Baltimore County Public Library: Video Library Network and American Library Association.

Del Vecchio, G. 1997. *Creating ever-cool: A marketer's guide to a kid's heart.* Gretna, LA: Pelican.

Fisher, P. H., and M. M. Pride. 2005. *Blueprint for your library marketing plan: A guide to help you survive and thrive.* Chicago: American Library Association.

Greene, J. O., and B. R. Burleson. 2003. *Handbook of communication and social interaction.* Mahwah, NJ: L. Erlbaum.

Horning, K. T. 1997. *From cover to cover: Evaluating and reviewing children's books.* New York: Harper Collins.

Janes, J. 2003. *Introduction to reference work in the digital age.* New York: Neal-Schuman.

Kids are patrons too! 1987. 15 min videocassette. Chicago: American Library Association.

McDaniel, J. A., and J. K. Ohles. 1993. *Training paraprofessionals for reference service.* New York: Neal-Schuman.

Riechel. R. 1991. *Reference services for children and young adults.* Hamden, CT: Shoe String Press.

Statz, S. R. 2003. *Public speaking handbook for librarians and information professionals.* Jefferson, NC: McFarland.

Walter, V. A. 2001. *Children and libraries: Getting it right.* Chicago: American Library Association.

Weingand, D. E. 1997. *Customer service excellence: A concise guide for librarians.* Chicago: American Library Association.

Willis, M. R. 1999. *Dealing with difficult people in the library.* Chicago: American Library Association.

Wolfe, L. A. 1997. *Library public relations, promotions, and communications.* New York: Neal-Schuman.

four

Materials and Collection Development

Knowledge of Materials

- Demonstrates a knowledge and appreciation of children's literature, periodicals, audiovisual materials, Websites and other electronic media, and other materials that constitute a diverse, current, and relevant children's collection.

- Keeps abreast of new materials and those for retrospective purchase by consulting a wide variety of reviewing sources and publishers' catalogs, including those of small presses; by attending professional meetings; and by reading, viewing, and listening.

- Is aware of adult reference materials and other library resources which may serve the needs of children and their caregivers.

Ability to Select Appropriate Materials and Develop a Children's Collection

- Evaluates and recommends collection development, selection, and weeding policies for children's materials consistent with the mission and policies of the parent library and the ALA Library Bill of Rights, and applies these policies in acquiring and weeding materials for or management of the children's collection.

- Acquires materials that reflect the ethnic diversity of the community, as well as the need of children to become familiar with other ethnic groups and cultures.

- Understands and applies criteria for evaluating the content and artistic merit of children's materials in all genres and formats.

- Keeps abreast of current issues in children's materials collections and formulates a professional philosophy with regard to these issues.

- Demonstrates a knowledge of technical services, cataloging and indexing procedures, and practices relating to children's materials.

Ability to Provide Customers with Appropriate Materials and Information

- Connects children to the wealth of library resources, enabling them to use libraries effectively.

- Matches children and their families with materials appropriate to their interest and abilities.

- Provides help where needed, respects children's right to browse, and answers questions regardless of their nature or purpose.

- Assists and instructs children in information gathering and research skills as appropriate.

- Understands and applies search strategies to give children full and equitable access to information from the widest possible range of sources, such as children's and adult reference works, indexes, catalogs, electronic resources, information and referral files, and interlibrary loan networks.

- Compiles and maintains information about community resources so that children and adults working with children can be referred to appropriate sources of assistance.

- Works with library technical services to guarantee that the children's collection is organized and accessed for the easiest possible use.

- Creates bibliographies, booktalks, displays, electronic documents, and other special tools to increase access to library resources and motivate their use.

W hen public libraries first developed in this country, children were not always welcomed. Children pushed their way into libraries, literally and figuratively. In those days, there was limited literature for young people, little understanding of the developmental importance of early childhood years, and certainly little concern for the library as a provider of basic literacy skills.

In the twenty-first century, we have a very different vision of serving youth. It begins with libraries providing books and other materials and programs to assist parents to become their children's first teachers. It continues as we provide books and other media that are developmentally appropriate for children through the middle school years.

Depending on community needs, most public libraries include some form of literacy development as a strategic direction. They offer formal programs for adults or children or provide a strong support framework for children and caregivers through children's collections and programs. We are part of the educational framework of our communities; we offer materials and programs that people can use throughout their lifetimes.

The children's collection in any public library allows for the development and maintenance of literacy skills. It provides resources for a broad and varied array of information and recreation materials to satisfy the needs of multiple age ranges and interest levels. The children's collection promotes an appreciation of art and literature and introduces other cultures, times, and lifestyles. It enables children to participate in flights of fancy and a wide variety of vicarious experiences. Each year literally thousands of new children's books are published, many more remain in print, and even those titles that have gone out of print maintain their place on the shelves. But often, shelf space is limited and budgets inadequate, so how does the selector make wise decisions?

In this chapter, we take a look at some of the essential issues involved in building a dynamic collection: choosing materials, weeding, working with technical services, and making the collection work. We also look at the collection as a resource.

Choosing Materials

Building and maintaining relevant collections of informational, recreational, and educational materials in their various formats to meet children's varying developmental and curriculum needs are at the core of the children's librarian's responsibilities. Despite the wide variety of media in the modern library, the root of the word *libris*—the book—is also the root of our profession—librarianship. Our main mission has not changed fundamentally over the millennia. Librarians build collections and help readers, researchers, and others access the information or literature they need.

The essence of what libraries are and do revolves around collections. The public continues to think of libraries primarily as a source of information and lenders of books and media. But library materials are also the basis around which the children's librarian builds programs and provides effective reference and readers' advisory services; second only to staff costs, the book and materials budget usually accounts for the largest percentage of the overall library budget.

Because these materials (and their processing and circulation) are your core business, it is wise to have a collection development policy or, at the very least, a collection development statement. This policy or statement should do the following:

1. Outline what types of materials make up your collection and why they are included in your collection.
2. Reflect your library's mission.
3. Provide you with the flexibility to discard what is no longer appropriate or timely.
4. Outline your general selection criteria.
5. State your library's position on intellectual freedom.

This materials selection statement may be designed just for your children's collection, or it may be part of the larger library policy. It is your guide in making decisions about what to include in your collection. It is an important public document, which, especially in the case of challenges to library material, helps you back up your professional judgment. Libraries may have different policies relating to different kinds of media, or they may include all formats in a single basic policy.

Material selection is one of the primary focuses of the children's librarian's job. In some libraries, on-site librarians do all or most of their own selection. Some library systems use a central purchasing process for most new materials. Even in those libraries, the local community librarians have responsibility for identifying replacement needs and ephemeral items such as paperbacks and magazines. They often provide input to the children's book selector by developing and maintaining ongoing profiles of the changing collection needs of their library and its users. In either case, children's librarians must know the material in the collection intimately. They must be well read in order to provide good public service.

A good materials selector is aware of the appropriate reviewing media. With a little experience, that selector learns which review sources are most dependable and consistent in meeting his or her specific evaluation needs. The best review sources assist the librarian in identifying materials that reflect local needs and cover the various types of materials in the collection. The children's librarian may also be responsible for preparing original reviews of new materials to make selection decisions, for publication, or to share with colleagues.

It is always important for a selector to read widely, in a variety of genres. The children's librarian must be aware that children have varying tastes and that a popular materials collection must reflect those tastes, from the most sophisticated to the mundane. The children's librarian must create a collection that reflects a variety of reading levels, languages, and formats that appeal to different users. As publishing trends and popular interests evolve, the librarian must be willing to offer customers topics or formats that may be new or interesting. Allow your adult interests and reference requests to help inform decisions about which current issues to include in the children's collection. Be as sure as you can that your collection reflects different viewpoints, especially regarding controversial issues.

It is also important to take a chance occasionally on something new or different. Self-censorship can be more insidious than censorship imposed on you by others. How do you know if you are self-censoring? When you refuse to purchase materials for fear that they will generate complaints, rather than making an informed decision based on reviews or your own best professional judgment, you are self-censoring.

Weeding

Weeding is just as important as acquiring in maintaining a good, usable, up-to-date collection. It is an integral part of collection development. There is a major difference between an archival collection and a living, changing public library collection. An archive by definition keeps its holdings essentially forever. To be useful, a public library collection must change with the times and customer needs.

No library has enough shelf space to allow it to buy and buy and buy and never have to discard to make room for new acquisitions. Packed and cluttered shelves deter browsing and may actually reduce easy access to current, popular materials. Books age. A very few become classics, but most simply become dated either in tone or in fact, their physical condition deteriorates, or they are in some other way superseded. When that happens, it is part of your professional responsibility to remove the materials from use and replace them with more accurate, more popular, or more attractive items.

Some libraries have formal policies about what is to be weeded and when, but weeding is an art as well as a science. It is difficult to make absolute rules that apply in every situation— beyond continually eliminating books and other media in poor condition. Incorrect or inaccurate information should be removed from the collection, especially in the hard or social sciences. But does a five- or ten-year age limit on physics books make sense when, for example, you have an older title (in good condition and with relatively modern-looking illustrations) on the basic principles of the lever? The physics of levers hasn't changed since ancient Greece. Yet other principles of physics, like string theory, may not even be mentioned in a title that is only a few years old.

When weeding nonfiction, your own interests may or may not help keep you abreast of new findings in the sciences or geography or other changing topics, but there are Internet sources that provide guidance. Or you can simply refer to a current reference book or website and do a little research before looking at the contents or index of the books in question.

Weeding fiction can be a more ticklish operation. It is possible to set guidelines for discarding nonfiction by publication date. But fiction or picture book classics may be twenty-five, fifty, or one hundred years old and continue to be popular, even beloved by new generations of children. Although you will still weed on the basis of a book's condition, you must be aware of such classics as H. A. Rey's *Curious George* series and mindful of literary classics such as *Little Women*, *The Tale of Peter Rabbit*, and modern classics by Sendak, Carle, Blume, and many other writers and illustrators.

Mid-list or general interest fiction may not circulate well without some introduction by the librarian, either through displays, booktalks, bibliographies, or "hand selling" as you respond to reader advisory requests. Some titles may circulate only occasionally, as they appear on teachers' booklists. It is important for the librarian to understand local patterns and special needs in order to weed effectively.

Circulation may be a good indicator of whether a book has lost its utility. If you look at circulation statistics in different parts of the collection, you will notice that books in some categories seem to go out a dozen times a year (usually picture books and easy readers), others circulate half as much, and others you think are important move only once or twice a year (these are often curriculum-related). Should you use the same requirements for weeding all parts of the collection? No. If you can figure out the appropriate *turnover rate* for each major area of the collection, you can use different standards for different media, topics, or areas of the collection.

USING TURNOVER RATES

Turnover rates are simply a mathematical ratio. Divide the number of volumes owned (either in the total collection or by category) by the number of circulations per year. If you have 2,000 picture books and the total picture book circulation is 20,000 per year, the average or turnover rate is 10. As you check through the collection, you see that some titles do better, some do worse, and some don't move at all. The shelf sitters need to go, and the titles with really high circulation rates probably need to be evaluated for condition, with additional copies purchased to satisfy popular demand. You may have 200 American history titles but find that their turnover rate is only 4 per year; obviously you will not use the same numerical value to weed in this area as you use in more popular areas, because the history circulation is based more on school requirements. But, unless you have an idea of the optimum turnover rate for the various parts of the collection, you will find it difficult to judge how to apply circulation as an aid to weeding.

Technical Services

Another important "behind the scenes" part of collection development involves technical services. Keep the channels of communication open with the technical services staff, so that if problems crop up (and they do), you can help develop procedures that work for you and the children. Cataloging and processing usually make our collections usable, but occasionally they create roadblocks for both librarians and customers. How an item is cataloged dictates its location on the shelf. Be observant; if an item is cataloged for placement in a location that makes it invisible to the potential user, work with your cataloging department to make the necessary changes or adjustments. This may be an issue for individual titles, for unique characteristics of children's books, or simply for general children's needs. Some examples are simplified cataloging, labeling "skinny books," and whether picture books need Dewey decimal numbers.

SUMMING UP THE BASIC
COLLECTION DEVELOPMENT GUIDELINES

- Have written policies for selection and deselection criteria.

- Use a variety of review sources.

- Develop a spending plan.

- Develop a weeding plan and use the results of your work to guide replacement orders.

- Know how to help children find information from a variety of sources (including electronic).

- Make strategic purchasing decisions on the basis of what is most important to your community.

- Use feedback from readers or available circulation statistics to justify budget requests.

- Keep the collection relevant to your customers and they will come back for more.

Making the Collection Work

Raganathan's famous dictum to provide the right book to the right child at the right time may not always be possible, but with modern electronic information sources at their fingertips, children's librarians should be able to provide required information in a timely fashion. Never forget, though, that the public library's collections should go beyond the basic provision of information.

Public library children's rooms provide a variety of educational, cultural, and recreational material for a wide range of ages and abilities. They hold materials that young customers *want* to read. This does not mean, however, that the library provides only popular materials or best sellers. Philosophically, it means that libraries encourage children's imaginations, their interests, and their curiosity. It implies that we have more wide-ranging collections than a school library, for example, which primarily contains curriculum support.

Local needs help determine the right proportions of the various parts of your collection. How much should be devoted to pure curriculum support? How much should be dedicated to various ages, like preschoolers, primary readers, middle schoolers? What nonfiction is needed to meet general interest inquiries? What should you offer in both fiction and nonfiction for recreational reading? Are resources for parents and other interested adults included? What media or languages other than English will you offer?

Demographics help determine the answers to many of these questions, but the general strategic direction of your library as well as budgets and space may place limits on what you collect. Luckily, electronic media can help even small libraries offer a wide variety of information sources. Don't forget, though, that except for licensed or purchased software like databases, much of the "free" material available on the Internet comes to us without the vetting process we use on print and other recorded material.

When libraries select books, periodicals, musical recordings, movies, and other materials, there is generally a review process in which staff or a media reviewer has read, listened to, or viewed the material. There is an implied authority represented by the author, the publisher, or distributor. But if reviewers feel the material is inaccurate or does not reflect community standards, the library can bypass it and provide alternative or more appropriate resources for patrons.

The Internet has opened a whole new arena as well as a new debate in the realm of children and information. Librarians traditionally use their collections of print materials to help children satisfy their information needs—for homework or general interest. The contemporary librarian is also responsible for teaching young researchers how to search effectively and how to be critical of the information they locate on the Internet.

To filter or not to filter—that is the question. Many members of the public think that, by using blocking software designed to filter pornography, violence, or "adult topics," the library can "protect" them or their children from inappropriate websites or information. If only it were that simple. No matter how good the software is, it cannot review the material for timeliness, accuracy, authority, or organization—all factors that the librarian's professional skills bring to other parts of the collection. The blocking software is only a mechanical filter of what someone else deems to be objectionable words or images. This highly charged political debate will continue, with library staff ultimately responsible to their governing bodies, until either the software improves or the Internet metamorphoses into a more regulated format.

The Collection as Resource

For many children, having a clean, attractive, warm place to study or meet friends after school is important. All children and most adults respond positively to a children's room or area that is colorful and well maintained. Collections are in this sense also part of the furniture. Their physical appearance—neatly shelved, edged, or displayed—becomes part of the decor.

The physical condition and presentation of the collections are important to how young customers perceive the library, the collection, and the librarians. A neat, well-organized collection with fresh, clean books on display gives a good impression to casual visitors and dedicated customers alike. As an extension of whatever display or merchandising techniques you use, bibliographies, bookmarks, web pathfinders, and other print material can also highlight parts of your collection. With desktop publishing, even small libraries can provide attractive lists, newsletters, signage, and other promotional materials.

The collection should also be, if not the source of programming, at least an adjunct to it. Many programs include stories, booktalks, or crafts that are directly dependent on books, but even pure entertainment like a visiting magician should be tied to the collection with appropriate displays in the meeting room or children's room. This teaches customers that the public library has a wide, maybe even unexpected, breadth of books and media tied to their hobbies and interests as well as their homework.

It cannot be repeated too often that, because we deal with a special genre—children's literature—to be good librarians we must read widely to find the appropriate materials to suit the varied needs of different ages, learning styles, and interests. This is a responsibility that lasts throughout one's career. To be effective at reference and even more so at readers' advisory, librarians must know their collections and their customers.

Younger children, especially, may think their librarian has read everything in the collection. That's an impossible task, but there are ways to familiarize yourself with a wide variety of books by reviewing new titles as they come into the collection. The following checklist may be useful as you make notes (either mental or written) on new titles and authors as you add them to the collection:

> *Look at the cover carefully.* How attractive is it? Who does it appeal to? If there is a jacket or verso blurb, read it.
>
> *Flip through the pages.* What's the reading level? What's the physical format like? Does it look readable and inviting? If there are illustrations, do they relate to the text on the same page? Are they captioned effectively?
>
> *Fiction only: Read a few pages.* Does the story flow well? Are the characters well drawn or stereo-

typical? Do the plot, pacing, and setting grab the reader?

Nonfiction only: Who is the appropriate audience? Will it be useful for assignments, for browsing, or both? Is the information well organized? Are there an index, table of contents, special features, or illustrations? Is the book up to date?

Does the physical size of the book make it inviting? Is it too heavy to lug around or read in bed? Is the print too small or tight to read easily?

Is the book age-appropriate? Will older kids reject it because it looks too childish? Will younger children and their adults be drawn to a title that looks to be for the young but contains mature content?

When you have an idea of the titles in the collection, you will find it much easier to match the right books with your customers. At the same time, as you browse through the new books, you will find materials to read in more detail for later use in booktalking, storytelling, preparing bibliographies, or other activities.

Answering reference questions is usually easier for most librarians than providing readers' advisory. Once the reference interview narrows down the exact type of information needed, the catalog, bibliographies, or just one's knowledge of the Dewey decimal system help you find appropriate nonfiction titles. But only by knowing the collection well can you match the reading level, interest level, and other personal factors with the recreational reader.

Since a readers' advisory inquiry can be even more vague than many reference questions, the readers' advisory interview can be even more important than the reference interview in finding the appropriate book:

Does the customer know what he wants?

Can you help the customer narrow the search by asking what she has read before? What does she particularly like? Which appeals to her most—characters, plot, setting, or genre?

What is the customer's reading level? Will high interest in the topic make slightly more difficult reading acceptable?

Is the reader looking for a title for an assignment or for leisure reading?

Go to the shelf with the reader and "hand sell" a few likely titles, then leave him alone to make the choice. If you see him leaving empty-handed, offer to make additional suggestions.

Our mission as children's librarians is to provide the first entry point for children, and often their caregivers, to "the University of the People"—as public libraries were once called. We should offer the best that is available to awaken their minds to informal and formal learning, and build collections that are also the focus of programs people remember fondly all their lives.

Suggested Reading

Before Collection Development

Larson, J., and H. Totten. 1998. *Model policies for small and medium public libraries.* New York: Neal-Schuman.

Nelson, S. 2001. *The new planning for results: A streamlined approach.* Chicago: American Library Association.

Nelson, S., and J. Garcia. 2003. *Creating policies for results: From chaos to clarity.* Chicago: American Library Association.

Walter, V. 1992. *Output measures for public library service to children: A manual of standardized procedures.* Chicago: American Library Association.

General Information

Alabaster, C. 2002. *Developing an outstanding core collection: A guide for libraries.* Chicago: American Library Association.

Baker, S. L. 2002. *The responsive public library: How to develop and market a winning collection*, 2d ed. Englewood, CO: Libraries Unlimited.

Evans, G. E. 2000. *Developing library and information center collections*, 4th ed. Englewood, CO: Libraries Unlimited.

Futas, E. 1995. *Collection development policies and procedures*, 3d ed. Phoenix, AZ: Oryx.

Children's Services

Benne, M. 1998. Children's collections. In *Principles of children's services in public libraries*, 2d ed., 114–150. Chicago: American Library Association.

Connor, J. G. 1990. *Children's library services handbook.* Phoenix, AZ: Oryx.

Fasick, A. M. 1991. *Managing children's services in the public library.* Englewood, CO: Libraries Unlimited.

Hughes-Hassell, S., and J. C. Mancall. 2005. *Collection management for youth: Responding to the needs of learners.* Chicago: American Library Association.

Intner, S., J. F. Fountain, and J. E. Gilchrist. 2005. *Cataloging correctly for kids: An introduction to the tools*, 4th ed. Chicago: American Library Association.

Peterson, S. 2002. Collection development. In *Children's services training manual.* Willows, CA: North State Cooperative Library System.

Steele, A. T. 2001. *Bare bones children's services: Tips for public library generalists.* Chicago: American Library Association.

Guides to Children's Materials

Cianciolo, P. 2000. *Informational picture books for children.* Chicago: American Library Association.

DeLong, J. A., and R. E. Schwedt. 1997. *Core collection for small libraries: An annotated bibliography of books for children and young adults.* Lanham, MD: Scarecrow.

Gillespie, J. T., and C. J. Naden. 2002. *Best books for children: Preschool through grade 6,* 7th ed. Westport, CT: Bowker.

Goldsmith, F. 2005. *Graphic novels now: Building, managing, and marketing a dynamic collection.* Chicago: American Library Association.

Huck, C. 2003. *Children's literature in the elementary school,* 8th ed. New York: McGraw-Hill.

Lima, C. W. 2001. *A to zoo: Subject access to children's picture books,* 6th ed. Westport, CT: Bowker.

Odean, K. 1997. *Great books for girls: More than 600 books to inspire today's girls and tomorrow's women.* New York: Ballantine.

———. 1998. *Great books for boys: More than 600 books for boys 2 to 14.* New York: Ballantine.

———. 2003. *Great books for babies and toddlers: More than 500 recommended books for your child's first three years.* New York: Ballantine.

Price, A., and J. Yaakov. 2001. *Children's catalog,* 18th ed. New York: Wilson.

Rasinski, T. V., and C. S. Gillespie. 1992. *Sensitive issues: An annotated guide to children's literature K–6.* Phoenix, AZ: Oryx.

Ritchey, V. H., and K. E. Puckett. 1992. *Wordless/almost wordless picture books: A guide.* Englewood, CO: Libraries Unlimited.

Sutherland. Z. 1997. *Children and books,* 9th ed. New York: Longman.

Thomas, J. L. 1992. *Play, learn, and grow: An annotated guide to the best books and materials for very young children.* Westport, CT: Bowker.

Multicultural Resources

Anderson, V. 1994. *Native Americans in fiction: A guide to 765 books for librarians and teachers, K–9.* Jefferson, NC: McFarland.

Dole, P. P. 1993. *Religious books for children: An annotated bibliography.* Portland, OR: Church and Synagogue Library Association.

Miller-Lachmann, L. 1992. *Our family, our friends, our world: An annotated guide to significant multicultural books for children and teenagers.* Westport, CT: Bowker.

New York Public Library. 1993. *Light a candle! The Jewish experience in children's books.* New York: New York Public Library.

Totten, H. L., and I. Wood. 1996. *Culturally diverse library collections for youth.* New York: Neal Schuman.

Wood, I. 1999. *Culturally diverse videos, audios, and CD-ROMs for children and young adults.* New York: Neal-Schuman.

Miscellaneous

Donavin, D. P. 1992. *Best of the best for children: Books, magazines, videos, audio, software, toys, travel.* New York: Random House.

Moss, J., and G. Wilson. 1992. *From page to screen: Children's and young adult books on film and video.* Detroit: Gale Research.

Richardson, S. 1991. *Magazines for children: A guide for parents, teachers, and librarians.* Chicago: American Library Association.

Rollins, D., and D. Helmer. 1996. *Reference sources for children's and young adult literature.* Chicago: American Library Association.

Volgliano, D. 1996. *Reference books for children's collections*, 3d ed. New York: New York Public Library.

Walker, B. J. 2005. *Librarian's guide to developing Christian fiction collections for children.* New York: Neal-Schuman.

five
Programming Skills

- Designs, promotes, executes, and evaluates programs for children of all ages, based on their developmental needs and interests and the goals of the library.

- Presents a variety of programs or brings in skilled resource people to present these programs, including storytelling, booktalking, book discussions, puppet programs, and other appropriate activities.

- Provides outreach programs commensurate with community needs and library goals and objectives.

- Establishes programs and services for parents, individuals and agencies providing child-care, and other professionals in the community who work with children.

Children's librarians in the public library do more original programming than their colleagues who serve other age groups, and they are well known both within the profession and among the general public for the skill sets behind the programming. Still, it is important to acknowledge how carefully planned, educationally appropriate, and well rehearsed these programs for children must be.

In this chapter we offer practical suggestions for designing and presenting the wide range of programs offered by most libraries. Because this topic is so well covered in the professional literature, the chapter's reading list is especially important for new practitioners. It offers "how to" titles for both beginners and experienced programmers to consult for ideas, techniques, and book and media titles. In what follows we explore why programming is such a major responsibility for children's librarians and how it introduces children and their caregivers to our collections and supports basic literacy acquisition as well.

An Introduction

In the Child Development Table presented in chapter 1, the "Library Applications" column refers to programs designed for each age level. Most of these are story-based in the broadest sense. Introducing words, rhyme, narrative structure, and a variety of story types is a common thread in library story programs—from lap-sits for infants to sophisticated formal storytelling for older children, and everything in between. Whether one uses narration; song; pictures in books, on flannelboards, or on drawing boards; or other media, story has primacy. Humans of all ages seem to learn better through narrative than through straight recitation of fact. In fact, storytelling may be one of the oldest art forms in every culture. People have used it to record history, to teach moral lessons and natural history, and to entertain and amuse all ages. Librarian-storytellers are part of a grand tradition.

Booktalking is another traditional library program used to introduce children to the content of library collections. Other standard presentations include arts and crafts programs, gardening programs, science demonstrations, poetry, writing, music and magic, puppetry, readers' theater, and creative dramatics. The list is extensive. All library programs, though, must have the goal of bringing children and library materials together. One of the ways library presentations of these programs differ from other agencies' presentations is in being book-based in some way. Even when conducting basic entertainment programs, like magic shows or film showings, it is essential to remind the audience that the library has books on those subjects. Simple displays of related materials are one way to do that. Listing a few library titles on a program flyer is another. Better yet is for the performer to "plug" a title or two as a source for the performance, whether it is a story, a craft book, or a musical recording.

Library programs also give the children's librarian an opportunity to model behaviors for parents and caregivers. In early childhood programs, a librarian presents developmentally appropriate books, songs, rhymes, and movement that help parents develop their child's vocabulary, motor skills, and reading readiness. Picture book programs can help teachers learn how to present picture books to groups or introduce poetry read aloud. These "lessons" are seldom overt, but by developing polished and effective presentation skills, by obviously entertaining *and* educating children, librarians can send a message that is certainly clear.

Since the mid-1970s, the emphasis of library programming has been on the early childhood audience. Before that time, only children mature enough to attend programs without a parent or caregiver, who could sit quietly in a group and listen to stories, were invited to "preschool storytime." The library's basic goal was to acculturate children to the behaviors needed to attend school.

As educational and psychological theory and practice evolved to prove how important the first few years of life are to future learning and school success, children's librarians turned their attention initially to three- and four-year-olds, then toddlers (one to two years), and even to infants. Because children often needed the comfort or assistance of an older companion, parents and caregivers were invited to the storytime programs as well. As children's librarians came to understand the importance of regular caregivers in a child's learning continuum, they began to incorporate subtle teaching or modeling behaviors into programs to help adults learn how to encourage children's learning at home, in the daycare setting, or wherever they interacted with those children. The caregiver's effect on the child is so much greater than a half-hour library program can be. Some librarians consider caregivers to be the primary audience for these programs.

Libraries also began to make parenting collections available right in the children's room so that adults who might not have time to browse could have access to materials on issues vital to their families. Brochures, bibliographies, and other kinds of print material were distributed not just in libraries but in maternity wards, WIC (Women's, Infants and Children) offices, clinics, and other places where parents and children were likely to congregate. Outreach for parents and story programs for children are also presented in community venues to attract new customers, share information, and raise awareness of the importance of library programs, materials, and services. This was the impetus for the ALSC/PLA's Every Child Ready to Read program.

Many surveys show that the public understands and appreciates the role the public library plays in these arenas. Story programs for young children as well as homework resources for school-age children are often the most visible and most appreciated services offered by the public library. This brings high visibility to the children's room and to the children's librarian.

In an era of changing demographics, free children's programs are an excellent way to introduce newcomers to the services provided in public libraries. Many of the countries our new immigrants come from do not have the same tradition of tax-supported free library service. They are often surprised and pleased to find out that libraries offer something for everyone and are a public service in the community. When programs of any kind are especially tailored to their needs—for example, in their language or about their own cultural traditions—the library's reputation is enhanced. Often the first approach people make to the library is on behalf of their children. When young children use libraries, their parents, older siblings, and caregivers are sure to follow. Highlighting a variety of languages and cultures also helps other children in the community understand human differences and builds tolerance.

Although each presenter has favorites among the wide range of programs and age groups, the library should schedule not just programs the staff members enjoy doing but programs appropriate for the demographics served—programs that make the biggest impact on the community.

Whether or not the children's librarian conducts a full survey of library customers to guide programming choices, she should already have an idea about the needs of the community. An area with lots of babies has different needs than a more mature neighborhood with working parents and school-age children. Where there are many young children, the obvious choices include baby lap-sits and toddler times. But both of these programs require or encourage participation by a parent or caregiver. In some areas most children are in daycare by their first birthday, so the children's librarian may choose to do the bulk of the early childhood presentations as on-site programs in the nursery schools or daycare centers, or to train their teachers to present book- or story-based programs in the classroom rather than have "family programs" in the library.

In neighborhoods with mostly school-age children, it will probably still be necessary to provide some in-library early childhood programming, but the library can concentrate on serving classes during the school day and providing out-of-schooltime activities for children ages five to twelve. A designated day and time may be set aside for parents and children to attend programs for the very young, or programs may be offered as limited series. For example, the baby program may be scheduled for four weeks, followed by a six- or eight-week toddler series, back to babies, and so on. This approach still leaves sufficient time to schedule classes or school visits on the other weekday mornings. Or, if staffing levels permit, early childhood programs can be presented on the weekends to encourage working parents to attend.

When the children's librarian begins work in a new location, she should use the existing or previous schedules as a guide, but it is important that she also evaluate the situation for possible changes to assure that current community needs are being met.

Keys to Good Presentation

The old joke goes, "How do you get to Carnegie Hall? Practice, practice, practice." And that is also how the new librarian becomes an accomplished program presenter. (It also helps to be a bit of a ham.)

The children in your audiences will respond to and reward your skill with their attention, their laughter, and other appropriate emotional responses, which is why programming is one of the most rewarding and enjoyable parts of being a children's librarian. Unfortunately, some librarians are so enamored of the programming side that they ignore the other necessary competencies that make a truly effective children's librarian. Remember, no matter how polished you are as a presenter, if you don't know your collection well you may miss the opportunity to connect the right child with the right books; to have the right books on hand, you have to pay attention to your collection development needs, and ultimately to all your other responsibilities.

This chapter's reading list includes many good titles that give particular tips and samples for each performance genre. Usually the advice boils down to the following points:

> Begin by selecting materials you like yourself. Your
> enthusiasm always comes across to the audience.

Prepare a detailed outline of the presentation (usually in writing).

Practice and rehearse until you can deliver the program, demonstration, or story fluidly.

Evaluate the audience reaction and adjust the program as needed.

Present programs whenever you have the chance to build up your repertoire, your confidence, and your skills.

Prepare a display of related materials or have extra circulating copies of your source materials so your audience can borrow and enjoy books and media based on the program.

Evaluating Your Program

Another key to strong programs is evaluation. We outline some formal methods in chapter 2, but informal evaluation can work as well. Ask yourself the following questions:

Did the audience seem to enjoy it? Did they laugh in the appropriate places? Were they watching or listening with concentration?

If this was part of a series, did the audience come back? Were some topics more popular than others?

Did children or adults in the audience compliment you after the program? Did they ask when you were doing another one? Did they offer suggestions for similar programs?

Did the displayed material circulate?

Could you tell from your audience's reactions when their attention was straying? Was it the material or your presentation that lost them? Did you make an

effort to mix the content and change the pace and
mood of the program?

Was there too much or too little repetition for this age
group?

Was the audience the appropriate size? Did you have
too many or too few people for this kind of presentation?

Did you attract the desired age group?

Was the space comfortable?

If you are honest with yourself, these and similar questions
will come naturally, and the answers will tell you how to
improve your program. Some of us need other evaluators to
help develop our skills. Another adult observer can point out
the flaws or weaknesses in a program and offer suggestions on
how to improve it. As with many other learning experiences, it
may take time to find your own style and pace, but with time,
effort, and repetition, most librarians learn to be pretty good
storytellers and booktalkers.

Developing Policy

What policies should the children's department develop to facilitate programming? Policies vary from program to program, but
in general the answers to the following questions may help you
decide what guidelines you need for general programs.

Who is the audience for this specific kind of program?
Are adults allowed or encouraged to come, or
children only?

Is required registration needed?

Are there age limits for the program? Are they based
on solid developmental principles?

Are outside groups encouraged to join the publicly pro-
moted programs, or must they be served separately?

What is the best audience size for this kind of programming?

If a non-library employee is the presenter, what kind of
contracts are necessary? What are the guidelines
for the presenter's self-advertisement or solicitation
of business or donations? What are the insurance
ramifications? How and how much should the presenter be paid?

What are your publicity needs, and how can you
recruit an audience?

How can you best cooperate with schools and other
community agencies to promote the library?

Although public libraries usually provide programs for
free, in some communities registration or materials
charges may be necessary. Is there a way to waive
these fees for children who cannot afford them, or
who come to the library without adults who might
otherwise pay for them?

If the library usually sells books or other media in con-
nection with adult programs, do you want to do the
same for children's programs?

Where will your programs be presented? Are there
issues like fire laws (for the size of the audience) or
other safety issues (e.g., outdoor venues) that need
to be addressed? How about accessibility?

Other practical issues that may have to be addressed
include whether children can leave the room and return,
whether you need other adults in the room to help with emer-
gencies, whether people can come in late, and whether audience size must be limited because of available space. These
issues may seem mundane, but they can adversely affect the
experience of the whole audience when not addressed.

Libraries have to consider another set of issues for working
with schools and other community groups:

What schools or agencies will you serve? In a large system, this may be by neighborhood, in other places by the tax base that pays for library service or by school district, for example.

Will the library pay for supplementary performers in these venues?

Will you set up different library card registration rules for children who come with classes? Will you still require parental signatures or proof of address? Will you supply blank registration forms in bulk? Can you do on-site registrations?

If other agencies offer honoraria to your library staff, may they keep them? Do they go to the library as donations?

Can library staff leave the library to provide programs at other venues?

Is it more effective to go where the audience members (children, teachers, parents) are or insist that they visit the library?

How often can you provide program time and space for groups and still maintain your other services? Can you offer different levels of service, such as return visits to only borrow and return books, to keep the library accessible to groups but use staff time wisely?

How often should the library contact the schools to offer programs? Do you offer programming to teachers or parent groups as well?

In larger systems, the library may be mandated to serve a certain geographic area, and the level of contact may be determined by system administrators. Smaller libraries may also have some of these questions settled by political forces beyond their control.

Programming for both the general public and for local schools and other child-serving agencies is an important part of the public library's general strategy for reaching out to the community. To be done well, it requires training, practice, and a general aptitude for presentation skills. Support from administrators who know the importance of a vital children's room to the community perception of their overall service is also a key factor in how well the children's room staff provides service.

A common problem experienced by children's librarians with managers who have never done this level of original programming is being given insufficient preparation time for their programs during the workday. Another common and very real complaint arises when time spent performing is not counted on the daily schedule in the same way time spent on a reference desk is. Both are basic, important public services. The fact that one librarian is using reference books or databases while the other uses picture books and puppets is immaterial; they are both providing a much-needed service to their customers. The children's manager must educate those who prepare schedules to allow sufficient preparation time for programs and for cleanup afterwards, and to credit the program time just as other public service time is credited.

The presentation skills one learns in the children's room are easily translated into presentation skills that can educate, entertain, or influence adult audiences as well. Many administrators who began their careers as children's librarians use their storytelling skills most effectively when addressing political bodies, trustees, or the media. These skills enable them to advocate more effectively for their libraries with foundations and regulatory agencies and brings greater respect to their colleagues who are still delivering basic core service to youngsters and their adults.

Suggested Reading

General Programming

Association for Library Service to Children Division. 1996. *Programming for young children: Birth through age five.* Chicago: American Library Association.

Bauer, C. F. 1983. *This way to books.* New York: H. W. Wilson.

Cianciolo, P. J. 1997. *Picture books for children*, 4th ed. Chicago: American Library Association.

DeSalvo, N. N. 1993. *Beginning with books: Library programming for infants, toddlers and preschool children.* Hamden, CT: Library Professional Publications.

Freeman, J. 1997. *Hi ho librario! Songs, chants, and stories to keep kids humming.* Bal Cynwyd, PA: Rock Hill Press.

Lima, C. W., and J. A. Lima. 2001. *A to zoo: Subject access to children's picture books*, 6th ed. New Providence, NJ: Bowker.

Mohrmann, G. 1994. *1001 rhymes and fingerplays.* Grand Rapids, MI: McGraw-Hill.

Nespeca, S. M., and J. B. Reeve. 2003. *Picture books plus: 100 extension activities in art, drama, music, math, and science.* Chicago: American Library Association.

Painter, W. M. 1989. *Musical story hours: Using music with storytelling and puppetry.* Hamden, CT: Library Professional Publications.

Reid, R. 2003. *Something funny happened on the way to the library: How to create humorous programs for children and young adults.* Chicago: American Library Association.

Robertson, D. A. 2005. *Cultural programming for libraries: Linking libraries, communities and culture.* Chicago: American Library Association.

Wadham, T. 1999. *Programming with Latino children's materials.* New York: Neal-Schuman.

Youth Services Division. 1993. *Programming on $1.98 a day.* New York: New York Library Association.

Book Discussions

Dodson, S., and T. Baker. 1996. *Mother-daughter book club: How ten busy mothers and daughters came together to talk, laugh, and learn through their love of reading.* New York: Harper Perennial.

Booktalking

Broman, J. 2001. *Booktalking that works.* New York: Neal-Schuman.

Littlejohn, C. 1999. *Talk that book! Booktalks that promote reading.* Worthington, OH: Linworth.

————. 2000. *Keep talking that book! Booktalks that promote reading,* vol. 2. Worthington, OH: Linworth.

Crafts

Faurot, K. K. 2003. *Books in bloom: Creative patterns and props that bring stories to life.* Chicago: American Library Association.

Gilbert, L. 2002. *50 great make-it and take-it projects.* Fort Atkinson, WI: UpstartBooks.

Lewis, A. 2002. *The jumbo book of paper crafts.* Toronto, ON: Kids Can Press.

Marks, D. F. 1996. *Glues, brews, and goos: Recipes and formulas for almost any classroom project.* Englewood, CO: Teacher Ideas Press.

Pavon, A., and D. Borrego. 2003. *25 Latino craft projects.* Chicago: American Library Association.

Totten, K. 1998. *Storytime crafts.* Fort Atkinson, WI: Alleyside Press.

————. 2002. *Seasonal storytime crafts.* Fort Atkinson, WI: UpstartBooks.

Family Programs

Nespeca, S. M. 1994. *Library programming for families with young children.* New York: Neal-Schuman.

Reid, R. 1999. *Family storytimes: Twenty-four creative programs for all ages.* Chicago: American Library Association.

Flannelboard Storytelling

Carlson, A. D., and M. Carlson. 1999. *Flannelboard stories for infants and toddlers.* Chicago: American Library Association.

————. 2005. *Flannelboard stories for infants and toddlers, bilingual edition.* Translated into Spanish by M. Pavon, M. Kramer, and I. Delgadillo-Romo for Bibliotecas Para La Gente. Chicago: American Library Association.

Lyn, D., and S. Hicks. 1997. *Flannelboard classic tales.* Chicago: Amcrican Library Association.

Marsh, V. 2002. *Stories that stick: Quick and easy storyboard tales.* Fort Atkinson, WI: Upstart books.

Sierra, J. 1997. *Flannelboard storytelling book*, 2d ed. New York: H. W. Wilson.

Infant and Toddler Programming

Acredolo, L., and S. Goodwyn. 2002. *Baby signs: How to talk with your baby before your baby can talk.* Chicago: Contemporary Books.

Daimant-Cohen, B. 2005. *Mother Goose on the loose.* New York: Neal-Schuman.

Davis, R. W. 1998. *Toddle on over: Developing infant and toddler literature programs.* Fort Atkinson, WI: Highsmith Press.

Ernst, L. 2001. *Lapsit services for the very young II.* New York: Neal-Schuman.

Feirerabend, J. M. 2000. *Bounces: Wonderful songs and rhymes passed down from generation to generation for infants and toddlers.* Chicago: GIA First Steps.

———. 2000. *Tapping and clapping: Wonderful songs and rhymes passed down from generation to generation for infants and toddlers.* Chicago: GIA First Steps.

———. 2000. *Wiggles and tickles: Wonderful songs and rhymes passed down from generation to generation for infants and toddlers.* Chicago: GIA First Steps.

Ghoting, S. N., and P. Martin-Diaz. 2005. *Early literacy storytimes @ your library: Partnering with caregivers for success.* Chicago: American Library Association.

Greene, E. 1991. *Books, babies, and libraries: Serving infants, toddlers, their parents and caregivers.* Chicago: American Library Association.

Jeffery, D. A. 1995. *Literate beginnings: Programs for babies and toddlers.* Chicago: American Library Association.

Marino, J. 2003. *Babies in the library.* Lanham, MD: Scarecrow Press.

Marino, J., and D. Houlihan. 1992. *Mother Goose time: Library programs for babies and their caregivers.* New York: H. W. Wilson.

Newcome, Z. 2002. *Head, shoulders, knees, and toes and other action rhymes.* Cambridge, MA: Candlewick Press.

Nichols, J. 1998. *Storytimes for two-year-olds*, 2d ed. Chicago: American Library Association.

Story-Huffman, R. 1996. *Nursery rhyme time.* Fort Atkinson, WI: Alleyside Press.

Preschool Storytime Programming

Benton, G., and T. Waichulaitis. 2003. *Ready-to-go storytimes: Fingerplays, scripts, patterns, music and more.* New York: Neal-Schuman.

Briggs, D. 1997. *52 programs for preschoolers: The librarian's year-round planner.* Chicago: American Library Association.

Broman, J. 2003. *Storytime action: 2000+ ideas for making 500 picture books interactive.* New York: Neal-Schuman.

Castellano, M. 2002. *Simply super storytimes: Programming ideas for ages 3–6.* Fort Atkinson, WI: UpstartBooks.

Cullum, C. N. 1990. *The storytime sourcebook: A compendium of ideas and resources for storytellers.* New York: Neal-Schuman.

Dixon, T. V., and P. Blough. 2006. *Sound of storytime.* New York: Neal-Schuman.

Sitarz, P. G. 1987. *Picture book story hours: From birthdays to bears.* Littleton, CO: Libraries Unlimited.

———. 1990. *More picture book story hours: From parties to pets.* Englewood, CO: Libraries Unlimited.

Puppetry

Anderson, D. 1997. *Amazingly easy puppet plays: 42 new scripts for one-person puppetry.* Chicago: American Library Association.

Bauer, C. F. 1997. *Leading kids to books through puppets.* Chicago: American Library Association.

Briggs, D. 1999. *101 fingerplays, stories, and songs to use with finger puppets.* Chicago: American library Association.

Champlin, C. 1998. *Storytelling with puppets.* Chicago: American Library Association.

Frey, Y. A. 2004. *One-person puppetry streamlined and simplified.* Chicago: American Library Association.

Lohnes, M. 2002. *Fractured fairy tales: Puppet plays and patterns.* Fort Atkinson, WI: UpstartBooks.

Marsh, V. 1998. *Puppet tales.* Fort Atkinson, WI: Alleyside Press.

Minkle, W. 1999. *How to do "The Three Bears" with two hands.* Chicago: American Library Association.

Pflomm, P. 1994. *Puppet plays plus: Hand puppet plays for two puppets.* Metuchen, NJ: Scarecrow.

Wright, D. 1990. *One-person puppet plays.* Englewood, CO: Teacher Ideas Press.

Readers' Theater

Barchers, S. I. 1997. *Fifty fabulous fables: Beginning readers theatre.* Englewood, CO: Teacher Ideas Press.

Bauer, C. F. 1987. *Presenting reader's theater: Plays and poems to read aloud.* New York: H. W. Wilson.

School-Age Programming

Bauer, C. F. 1985. *Celebrations: Read aloud holiday and theme book programs.* New York: H. W. Wilson.

Cook, S., F. Corcoran, and B. Fonnesbeck. 2001. *Battle of the books and more: Reading activities for middle school students.* Fort Atkinson, WI: Highsmith.

Fiore, C. 1998. *Running summer library reading programs.* New York: Neal-Schuman.

―――. 2005. *Fiore's summer library reading program handbook.* New York: Neal-Schuman.

Johnson, W. L., and Y. C. Johnson. 1999. *Summer reading program fun: 10 thrilling, inspiring, wacky board games for kids.* Chicago: American Library Association.

Raines, S. C., and R. J. Canady. 1989. *Story stretchers: Activities to expand children's favorite books.* Mt. Rainier, MA: Gryphon House.

―――. 1991. *More story stretchers: Activities to expand children's favorite books.* Mt. Rainier, MA: Gryphon House.

Reid, R. 2004. *Cool story programs for the school-age crowd.* Chicago: American Library Association.

Simpson, M. S., and L. Perrigo. 2001. *Storycraft: 50 theme-based programs combining storytelling, activities, and crafts for children in grades 1–3.* Jefferson, NC: McFarland.

Sitarz, P. G. 1997. *Storytime sampler: Read alouds, booktalks, and activities for children.* Littleton, CO: Libraries Unlimited.

Stassevitch, V., P. Stemmler, R. Shotwell, and M. Writh. 1998. *Ready-to-use activities for before and after school programs.* West Nyack, NY: Center for Applied Research in Education.

Vardel, S. M. 2006. *Poetry aloud here! Sharing poetry with children in the library.* Chicago: American Library Association.

Storytelling

Bauer, C. F. 1993. *Caroline Feller Bauer's new handbook for storytellers: With stories, poems, magic, and more.* Chicago: American Library Association.

Cooper, C. H. 1998. *The storyteller's cornucopia.* Fort Atkinson, WI: Alleyside Press.

De Wit, D. 1979. *Children's faces looking up: Program building for the storyteller.* New York: Neal-Schuman.

Greene, E. 1996. *Storytelling: Art and technique,* 3d ed. New Providence, NJ: Bowker.

Haven, K. 2000. *Super simple storytelling: A can-do guide for every classroom, everyday.* Englewood, CO: Teacher Ideas Press.

MacDonald, M. R. 1994. *Celebrate the world: Twenty tellable folktales for multicultural festivals.* New York: H. W. Wilson.

———. 2004. *Audience participation folktales for the beginner storyteller.* Chicago: American Library Association.

———. 2004. *Twenty tellable tales: Audience participation folktales for the beginning storyteller.* Chicago: American Library Association.

Marsh, V. 1996. *Storyteller's sampler.* Fort Atkinson, WI: Alleyside Press.

Pellowski, A. 1984. *The story vine: A source book of unusual and easy-to-tell stories from around the world.* New York: Macmillan.

———. 1990. *The world of storytelling,* exp. rev. ed. New York: Macmillan.

Sawyer, R. 1962. *The way of the storyteller.* New York: Viking.

Sierra, J. 1996. *Storytellers' research guide: Folktales, myths, and legends.* Eugene. OR: Folkprint.

Sierra, J., and R. Kaminski. 1991. *Multicultural folktales: Stories to tell young children.* Phoenix, AZ: Oryx.

six

Advocacy, Public Relations, and Networking Skills

- Promotes an awareness of and support for meeting children's library and information needs through all media.

- Considers the opinions and requests of children in the development and evaluation of library services.

- Ensures that children have full access to library materials, resources, and services as prescribed by the Library Bill of Rights.

- Acts as liaison with other agencies in the community serving children, including other libraries and library systems.

- Develops cooperative programs between the public library, schools, and other community agencies.

- Extends library services to children and groups of children presently unserved.

- Utilizes effective public relations techniques and media to publicize library activities.

- Develops policies and procedures applying to children's services based on federal, state, and local law where appropriate.

- Understands library governance and the political process and lobbies on behalf of children's services.

In earlier chapters we discussed many of the issues included in this competency because advocating for children and their services is so basic and integral to what we do as children's librarians. We explored being a player and a partner in the child-serving community of other professionals, reaching out to other members of the service community to advertise our services or connect our patrons to theirs, and bringing more visibility to the library. In this chapter we reexamine these issues and also look at several political issues relevant to children's librarianship—including intellectual freedom and child-friendly policies and procedures. We explore the role of public relations and how making the right connections can benefit the library and make funders, public and private, look good as well, which in turn allows us to provide both core and special services needed in our communities.

Briefly, let us recap the main points about the advocacy and networking roles of the children's librarian discussed in previous chapters:

Children's librarians must speak for the child customer within the library.

Children's librarians are advocates for services to parents, teachers, and other caregivers.

In a large department or a system, the children's manager speaks for the staff.

The children's librarian who forms an alliance with young adult or teen librarians can be a stronger voice for youth.

A good librarian listens to the concerns and requests of the customers and adapts programs and services to their needs.

Children's librarians seek to ensure that their library administration allocates resources (budget and staff) to support the needs of children and families in their communities adequately.

Children's librarians ensure that policies and procedures for library service to children are free, open, accessible, and equitable to children and families.

An outside advocacy role helps the librarian find colleagues in the community who serve a similar advocacy role in support of children and families.

When other professionals working with children feel isolated or sidelined in their agencies, the children's librarian can provide support.

It helps to develop a network of colleagues—daycare providers, teachers, medical pediatric specialists—who serve the same customer base.

Active membership in professional librarian groups, unions, or community groups raises the visibility of children's library services and staff and makes the children's librarian a "player," one whom others consult on issues relating to children, literacy, and library issues.

Parents form an important part of the children's librarian's constituency, and family programs are an important mechanism to familiarize them with what the public library can do for their children. Because library programs and services are generally free of charge, we can serve the whole community.

Show us the money! High visibility helps at budget time, whether inside the library or in the election process when voters decide on tax support. Grant opportunities are often more readily available when community groups apply in partnership. A vocal, supportive customer base helps children's services argue for a fair share of funding within the library administration as well.

Children's librarians can play an important role in the political process. Visibility is essential at budget

> time, whether it is local government funding or internal budget allocations. In any election process for libraries that goes directly to the voters for support, visibility and publicizing the benefits the library provides for children and families are essential.

Libraries have not always sought publicity or new customers. Library administrators tended to assume that, because libraries were traditional institutions and considered providers of a "worthy" service, offering good books and educational programs to all, they were sacrosanct and immune from fiduciary scrutiny. But when economic times got tight and libraries had to compete for funding with municipal health, safety, recreation, cultural, and educational departments, suddenly being "worthy" was not enough. The library had to justify its worth and show active community involvement in order to maintain budget support. We learned to use advocacy, networking, and public relations the hard way.

Savvy library directors learned that everyone loves children and used this lesson to good effect. Politicians and grant donors love to have their pictures taken with cute kids. Reporters and editors can always find a human interest angle in stories about services to children and their families. And parents and grandparents vote for programs that support them. Other librarians began to develop a new respect for how the children's department could bring visibility and funds to the library. Outreach, simply defined as making connections to other agencies and bringing the library's programs and services to the attention of new audiences, took on a higher priority.

For most children's librarians who already worked with schools, daycare agencies, or other community groups serving children, outreach was an integral part of their service. What was, and still is, distressing is the lack of recognition of the public library as a community resource and its role in disseminating information across broad demographic categories. Now, thanks to the ongoing efforts of children's librarians among other activist librarians, the tide is beginning to turn, and other agencies covet our audience. Museums, for example, marvel at the voluntary but strong support displayed by our users. In many areas, especially where funding sources demand cooperative efforts between agencies, the library is now considered to be an ideal partner for reaching variously defined underserved populations: families of preschool children, the poor, people on the wrong side of the "digital divide," the elderly, immigrants, and many other demographic constituencies.

If any library administrator still doubts the potency of a well-designed outreach strategy, she need only look at the professional media. The journals are full of examples of successful programs for political action, of strategies for raising funds (both public and private) and reaching new audiences. Where the library is a vital part of the community, it is so because it reaches into the community and responds to its informational, recreational, and educational needs.

In some communities, local media are anxious to include news about library events or good books to read in their neighborhood or local events columns. Programs, services, and collections for children are often highlighted in this way, and the library may even find corporate partners who include the library in their advertising or fund advertising for specific programs they support.

Radio and television outlets may also broadcast library public service announcements or include library spokespeople in local programming. Depending on the size of the library and local media opportunities, librarians may or may not be directly involved in placing, writing, or appearing in stories or advertising. But even in large systems with special public relations or marketing departments, children's services staff are frequently called upon to demonstrate to the community's leaders the work they do for their constituents.

Advocacy can also take on many other forms, from a conversation in the supermarket line to visits to local, state, or national politicians. It is useful to have a few ready remarks and some basic facts always prepared for such occasions: How does reading during summer vacation encourage children's reading ability overall? How does free voluntary reading improve their ability to do well on standardized tests? How many nursery schools and daycare centers are served by your library? How does your library help families? How does an investment in educational programs for children pay off for the community? And there will be many other facts that appeal specifically to the needs of your customers, supporters, and politicians.

Those of us who care about children must also care about their rights as citizens. Intellectual freedom issues such as access to information and appropriate materials, the right to privacy, and equality under our policies and procedures at the library also fall within the purview of children's librarians. The issues of censorship and intellectual freedom are sensitive ones. From a professional standpoint, our goal is to remain steadfast to the tenets of the First Amendment as they pertain to children as well as to adults. At the same time, it is important to remember that we live and work in an environment in which many adults feel that children must be protected from ideas and information some consider harmful. Well before the Internet era, well-meaning adults challenged library materials. Regardless of ideology, concerned adults and ideologues of all persuasions seek to "protect" children from facts, thoughts, words, or illustrations they deem inappropriate. The availability of public access computers in public libraries has only exacerbated the situation.

Children's services must work with the administration to develop policies and procedures for handling complaints about library materials. That is why it is essential to have written collection development and materials selection policies or statements. It is important to have strongly worded Internet use policies and procedures to handle situations with both adult and child users. It is also important for the library to develop "scripts" as ready responses for customers who are viewing inappropriate websites, or for customers who complain about other users in the library.

Many well-meaning adults are tempted to legislate protections for children without fully understanding the issues. This may be as simple as a customer contacting a local government official to complain about a book, or it can be as complex as federal, state, or local legislation limiting Internet access by age. It is important for librarians to understand and defend First Amendment rights for their users of all ages. Many youth services librarians have testified in local hearings, in court battles, and in the media for the right of youngsters to unfettered access to information, because a commitment to the public's "right to know" is one of the founding tenets of our service philosophy.

For those of us who work with children, there is a fine line between selection of appropriate material and censorship. There is no easy way to define when one crosses that line and denies access to some material simply because it conflicts with community standards or our own personal taste.

It has been said that a library that has nothing in it that makes its own staff uncomfortable is a library that is not doing its job. Children need to learn many things, some of which make adults uncomfortable, before they can mature into good citizens. Giving children access to the information and ideas they need to explore is part of the librarian's job. Each of us must make controversial choices from time to time for our young customers, but if we have a strong, well-designed policy to help us make those decisions, the controversy can be minimized. Still, it is wise to remember that as an employee of an organization you are responsible for explaining and upholding the policies and procedures of that organization. If you do not agree with them, you must either come to terms with the policy and uphold it graciously or seriously consider removing yourself from that organization and finding a more congenial work situation.

Suggested Reading

Allen, M. L. 1995. Networking and cooperation. In *Youth services librarians as managers: A how-to guide from budgeting to personnel*, ed. K. Staerkel, M. Fellows, and S. M. Nespeca. Chicago: American Library Association.

Ball, S., comp. 2003. *Know kidding: The best of the best in youth services.* Wheeling, IL: North Suburban Library System.

Fasick, A. L. 1998. Community public relations. In *Managing children's services in the public library*, 2d ed., 151–163. Englewood, CO: Libraries Unlimited.

———. 1998. Networking with other children's librarians. In *Managing children's services in the public library*, 2d ed., 193–202. Englewood, CO: Libraries Unlimited.

Ghoting, S. N., and P. Martin-Diaz. 2005. *Early literacy storytimes @ your library: Partnering with caregivers for success.* Chicago: American Library Association.

Karp, R. S., ed. 1995. *Part time public relations with full time results: A PR primer for libraries.* Chicago: American Library Association.

Kids can't wait. 1996. 8 min., 35 sec. videocassette. Chicago: American Library Association.

Osborne, R., ed. 2004. *From outreach to equity: Innovative models of library policy and practice.* Chicago: American Library Association.

Pfeil, A. B. 2005. *Going places with youth outreach: Smart marketing strategies for your library.* Chicago: American Library Association.

Robertson, D. A. 2005. *Cultural programming for libraries: Linking libraries, communities and culture.* Chicago: American Library Association.

Siess, J. A. 2003. *The visible librarian: Asserting your value with marketing and advocacy.* Chicago: American Library Association.

Turner, A. M. 1997. *Getting political: An action guide for librarians and library supporters.* New York: Neal-Schuman.

Wolfe, L. A. 2005. *Library public relations, promotions, and communications,* 2d ed. New York: Neal-Schuman.

Ziarnak, N. R. 2003. *School and public libraries: Developing the natural alliance.* Chicago: American Library Association.

seven

Professionalism and Professional Development

■ Acknowledges the legacy of children's librarianship, its place in the context of librarianship as a whole, and past contributions to the profession.

■ Keeps abreast of current trends and emerging technologies, issues, and research in librarianship, child development, education, and allied fields.

■ Practices self-evaluation.

■ Conveys a nonjudgmental attitude toward patrons and their requests.

■ Demonstrates an understanding of and respect for diversity in cultural and ethnic values.

■ Knows and practices the American Library Association's Code of Ethics.

■ Preserves confidentiality in interchanges with patrons.

■ Works with library educators to meet needs of library school students and promote professional association scholarships.

■ Participates in professional organizations to strengthen skills, interact with fellow professionals, and contribute to the profession.

■ Understands that professional development and continuing education are activities to be pursued throughout one's career.

In the public library, good librarians understand the communities they serve. They respect the cultural and ethnic diversity found in their local area, but they also help patrons understand the larger world around them. As intermediaries for library users between the user's request for information and the sources for it, we ask questions to clarify the search strategy, not to make value judgments about why or how the customer will make use of information. We make rules and policies that offer equity of service to all, but we adapt those rules as necessary to allow the public access to the information we hold for them.

Over the past century, there have been many role models, mentors, and innovators in service to children in public libraries. They have set the standard for exemplary service, professional development, and adapting the technologies, programmatic goals, and general library services to our young patrons.

Virginia Walter, past president of ALSC and leading educator, postulates "Five Laws of Children's Librarianship" in her book *Children and Libraries: Getting It Right* (2001). We cite these postulates here because they summarize so well what children's librarians try to accomplish every day.

> Libraries serve the reading interests and information needs of all children, directly and through service to parents and other adults who are involved with the lives of children.
>
> Children's librarians provide the right book or information for the right child at the right time in the right place.
>
> Children's librarians are advocates for children's access to books, information, information technology, and ideas.
>
> Children's librarians promote children's literacy in all media.
>
> Children's librarians honor their traditions and create the future.

To serve children and their adults well, children's librarians need the same basic expertise as our colleagues who serve other age groups. They also need expertise in the literature for youth and in delivering age-appropriate and developmentally appropriate programming to youngsters. Although we can develop these skills and keep abreast of new information as individuals, joining with colleagues and sharing ideas through various professional venues and organizations makes it so much more enjoyable.

There are many ways to get involved with professional colleagues. Membership and participation in local, state, regional, and national organizations are available to us from the time we attend graduate school, through our active careers, and even into retirement if we so choose.

Subscribing to and reading library, educational, book-review, and general adult media help us in our daily jobs. Serving on committees, whether in the workplace or in a professional association, can bring a great deal of satisfaction and a sense of giving back to the profession. Mentoring new librarians and sharing the lessons and expertise one has developed are also highly rewarding for both individuals.

Political activism suits some people and also serves the profession and our customers by ensuring funds, legal rights, and a focus on intellectual freedom issues in venues outside of the library.

Librarians are, by and large, a friendly lot. If you work in a small library and need other colleagues to exchange ideas with, or even as you get to a high management position in a large library system and feel the need for a periodic reminder of why you love this profession, conventions and conferences offer a chance to meet new people, discover new ideas, and see new sights. Outsiders would be shocked, based on the old sensible shoe-bun-and-glasses stereotype, at how much noise and fun librarians create at social events in conference after-hours.

Even if physical attendance at a conference is not in your budget, virtual attendance is a new option we can all take advantage of. Many state, regional, and national organizations now offer committee memberships to virtual members who are willing to work on a project but cannot travel long distances to meet. Issue- and interest-based electronic discussion lists allow librarians of varying levels to share ideas and expertise as well.

More than a century of public library service to children has moved us from the nurturing role of providing first educational, then recreational materials and services to school-age children, to service to parents and caregivers, and now to a full range of professional service for children from birth to middle school, along with their adults. In this book we attempt to help those looking at the complex role of the children's librarian to understand how the various skills, interests, and talents must blend in the individual librarian, who then adapts to the organizational structure he or she is working in to provide exemplary service, and ultimately to further the traditions of librarianship by mentoring other librarians.

At some time in your career, and depending on the size of your library, you may be responsible for training other librarians. To train or mentor others, we suggest, you should prepare a written plan, allow flexibility and experimentation (since we often learn the most from mistakes), and pass on not only specific methodologies but also the joy of working with children and a serious commitment to personally directed professional growth.

Children's librarianship is not for the lazy, the faint of heart, or the complacent. Children will challenge you intellectually, socially, and frequently. They will keep you young at heart, and you will have to make an effort to keep up with their new literature, new fads, new music, and new ideas. You may have to play "cop" at the beginning of each school year until the children understand proper library behavior, but you will also have the wonderful experience of opening the joys of reading to new generations of babies, toddlers, and parents. Children's librarianship provides a challenging and rewarding career as well as a tremendous stepping stone along other career pathways. The faces, the names, the stories, will stay with you for a lifetime. And perhaps you too will one day tell new librarians, "Everything I needed to know I learned in the Children's Room."

Suggested Reading

Albritton, R. L., and T. W. Shaughnessey. 1990. *Developing leadership skills: A source book for librarians.* Englewood, CO: Libraries Unlimited.

Benne, M. 1991. Professional role and responsibilities of the children's librarian. In *Principles of children's services in public libraries*, 329–363. Chicago: American Library Association.

Colorado Council for Library Development. 1997. *Diversity tool kit.* Denver: Colorado Council for Library Development.

Diversity in the library. 2001. 20 min. videocassette. Townsend, MD: Library Video Network.

Fasick, A. M. 1998. Networking with other children's librarians. In *Managing children's services in the public library*, 2d ed., 193–202. Englewood, CO: Libraries Unlimited.

Fellows, M. 1995. Continuing Education. In *Youth services librarians as managers: A how-to guide from budgeting to personnel*, ed. K. Staerkel, M. Fellows, and S. M. Nespeca. Chicago: American Library Association.

Long, H. G. 1969. *Public library service to children: Foundation and development.* Metuchen, NJ: Scarecrow.

Minow, M., and T. A. Lipinski. 2003. *The library's legal answer book.* Chicago: American Library Association.

Office of Intellectual Freedom. 2002. *Intellectual freedom manual*, 6th ed. Chicago: American Library Association.

Ross, C. S. 1998. *Communicating professionally: A how-to-do-it manual for library applications*, 2d ed. New York: Neal-Schuman.

Simpson, C. 2003. *Ethics in school librarianship: A reader.* Worthington, OH: Linworth.

Walter, V. A. 2001. *Children and libraries: Getting it right.* Chicago: American Library Association.

RELATED WEBSITES

One: Knowledge of Client Group

Americans with Disabilities Act
  www.usdoj.gov/crt/ada/adahom1.htm

Childbirth.Org
  www.childbirth.org/

Every Child Ready to Read
  www.pla.org/ala/pla/plaissues/earlylit/earlyliteracy.htm

Home School World
  www.home-school.com/

Know Kidding
  www.nsls.info/resources/knowkidding (Section 2:
  Linking Collections to Clients)

Zero to Three
  www.zerotothree.org/

Two: Administrative and Management Skills

Child Safety on the Information Highway
  www.safekids.com/child_safety.htm

Know Kidding
  www.nsls.info/resources/knowkidding (Section 1:
  Organizational Core, and Appendix 1: Policies)

Librarian's Index to the Internet
  lii.org/

Three: Communication Skills

Know Kidding
www.nsls.info/resources/knowkidding (Section 3: Communication)

Four: Materials and Collection Development

Book Links
www.ala.org/BookLinks/index.html

Booklist
www.ala.org/booklist/index.html

Bulletin of the Center for Children's Books
www.lis.uiuc.edu/puboff/bccb/

Cooperative Children's Book Center
www.soemadison.wisc.edu/ccbc/

Horn Book
www.hbook.com/index.shtml

School Library Journal
www.schoollibraryjournal.com/

Vandergrift's Children's Literature Page
www.scils.rutgers.edu/~kvander/

Five: Programming Skills

Carol Hurst Children's Literature Site
www.carolhurst.com/

Gayle's Preschool Rainbow
www.preschoolrainbow.org/preschool-rhymes.htm

Jan Brett's Web Page
www.janbrett.com/

Know Kidding
www.nsls.info/resources/knowkidding (Section 4: Programming)

Picturing Books
www.geocities.com/dimatulka/

The Puppetry Home Page
www.sagecraft.com/puppetry/

Whatcom County Library System
www.wcls.org/pdf_files/youththemebook.pdf

Six: Advocacy, Public Relations, and Networking Skills

American Association of School Librarians
www.ala.org/aasl/

Children's Book Council
www.cbcbooks.org/

Children's Defense Fund
www.childrensdefense.org/

Know Kidding
www.nsls.info/resources/knowkidding (Appendix 3:
Important Documents)

National Association for the Education of Young Children
www.naeyc.org/

Seven: Professionalism and Professional Development

Association for Library Service to Children
www.ala.org/alsc/

Public Library Association
www.pla.org/

Young Adult Library Services Association
www.ala.org/yalsa/

appendix
B
ALSC COMMITTEES AS THEY RELATE TO ALSC COMPETENCIES

One: Knowledge of Client Group

Library Service to Special Population Children and Their Caregivers (Priority Group I)

Preschool Services and Parent Education (I)

Preschool Services Discussion Group (I)

School-Age Programs and Service (I)

Intellectual Freedom (I)

Legislation (I)

Social Issues Discussion Group (I)

Great Websites (II)

ALSC/Book Wholesalers Summer Reading Program Grant and Reading Program (III)

Research and Development (V)

Liaison with National Organizations Serving Children (VII)

Public Library-School Partnerships Discussion Group (VII)

Children and Technology (VIII)

Education (VIII)

Two: Administrative and Management Skills

Organization and Bylaws (Priority Group IV)

Planning and Budget (IV)

Program Coordinating (IV)
Preconference Planning (IV)
Research and Development (V)
Managing Children's Services (VIII)
Education (VIII)
Managing Children's Services Discussion Group (VIII)
Children's Book (Collection Development) Discussion
    Group (VIII)

Three: Communication Skills

Library Service to Special Population Children and Their
    Caregivers (Priority Group I)
Preschool Services and Parent Education (I)
Preschool Services Discussion Group (I)
School-Age Programs and Service (I)
Intellectual Freedom (I)
International Relations (I)
Legislation (I)
Publications (V)
Oral History (V)
Liaison with National Organizations Serving Children (VII)
Public Library-School Partnerships Discussion Group (VII)
Managing Children's Services (VIII)
Education (VIII)
Managing Children's Services Discussion Group (VIII)
Storytelling Discussion Group (VIII)

Four: Materials and Collection Development

Library Service to Special Population Children and Their
    Caregivers (Priority Group I)
Social Issues Discussion Group (I)
Intellectual Freedom (I)

Preschool Services and Parent Education (I)

Preschool Services Discussion Group (I)

School-Age Programs and Service (I)

Great Websites (II)

Notable Books (II)

Notable Recording (II)

Notable Video (II)

Notable Computer Software (II)

Collections of Children's Books for Adult Research Discussion Group (V)

National Planning of Special Collections (V)

Batchelder Award (VI)

Belpré Award (VI)

Caldecott Award Selection (VI)

Carnegie Award Selection (VI)

Newbery Award Selection (VI)

Sibert Informational Book Award (VI)

Wilder Selection (VI)

Children's Book (Collection Development) Discussion Group (VIII)

Managing Children's Services (VIII)

Children and Technology (VIII)

Education (VIII)

Quick Lists Consulting Group

Five: Programming Skills

Library Service to Special Population Children and Their Caregivers (Priority Group I)

Preschool Services and Parent Education (I)

Preschool Services Discussion Group (I)

School-Age Programs and Service (I)

Program Coordinating (IV)

Managing Children's Services (VIII)
Managing Children's Services Discussion Group (VIII)
Storytelling Discussion Group (VIII)
Education (VIII)

Six: Advocacy, Public Relations, and Networking Skills

Library Service to Special Population Children and Their Caregivers (Priority Group I)
Preschool Services and Parent Education (I)
Preschool Services Discussion Group (I)
School-Age Programs and Service (I)
Intellectual Freedom (I)
International Relations (I)
Legislation (I)
Social Issues Discussion Group (I)
Liaison with National Organizations Serving Children (VII)
Public Library-School Partnerships Discussion Group (VII)
Education (VIII)
Managing Children's Services (VIII)

Seven: Professionalism and Professional Development

International Relations (Priority Group I)
ALSC/Book Wholesalers Summer Reading Program Grant and Reading Program (III)
ALSC/Econo-Clad Literature Program Award (III)
Arbuthnot Honor Lecture (III)
Bechtel Fellowship (III)
Distinguished Service Award (III)
Penguin Putnam Books for Young Readers Award (III)
Scholarships: Melcher and Bound to Stay Bound (III)
Local Arrangements (IV)
Membership (IV)

Nominating (IV)
Preconference Planning (IV)
Program Coordinating (IV)
Children and Libraries Editorial Advisory (VIII)
Children and Technology (VIII)
Children's Book Discussion Group (VIII)
Education (VIII)
Managing Children's Services (VIII)
Managing Children's Services Discussion Group (VIII)
Storytelling Discussion Group (VIII)

INDEX

Rosanne Cerny is a native New Yorker. She got her MLS from Rutgers University, and after beginning her career in suburban New Jersey moved on to the New York Public Library and then to the Queens Library. She has worked in New York City since 1970 in a variety of positions, in four of the five boroughs, and she has been Coordinator of Children's Services at the Queens Library since 1992. She is active in ALA/ALSC, PLA, and the New York Library Association. She is an adjunct instructor at Queens College Graduate School of Library and Information Studies.

Penny S. Markey is Coordinator of Youth Services for the County of Los Angeles Public Library. In addition to overseeing the training of children's services staff, she plans, implements, and evaluates library programs and services for children and young people and their families. She has served on the ALSC board and the ALA council. She has participated in numerous ALSC committees and has served as chair of the ALSC Managing Children's Services Committee. She is an adjunct professor in the Department of Education and Information Science at the University of California, Los Angeles, where she teaches classes on library services and programs for children. She is the recipient of the 2003 ALA Grolier Award for her contribution to the field of library service for children.

Amanda Jane Williams, PhD, lives in Austin, Texas, and currently works for the Austin Public Library at the Little Walnut Creek Branch. Over the past twenty-five years, Dr. Williams has worked in support of library service to children as a children's librarian for the Dallas Public Library in Dallas, Texas, as the youth services consultant for the Central Texas Library System, and now as a branch librarian. For the past fifteen years she has taught children's literature to undergraduate students for the School of Information at the University of Texas at Austin.